KINSHIP AND SOCIAL ORGANIZATION

LONDON SCHOOL OF ECONOMICS
MONOGRAPHS ON SOCIAL ANTHROPOLOGY

Managing Editor: Anthony Forge

The Monographs on Social Anthropology were established in 1940 and aim to publish results of modern anthropological research of primary interest to specialists.

The continuation of the series was made possible by a grant in aid from the Wenner-Gren Foundation for Anthropological Research, and more recently by a further grant from the Governors of the London School of Economics and Political Science. Income from sales is returned to a revolving fund to assist further publications.

The Monographs are under the direction of an Editorial Board associated with the Department of Anthropology of the London School of Economics and Political Science.

LONDON SCHOOL OF ECONOMICS
MONOGRAPHS ON SOCIAL ANTHROPOLOGY
No. 34

KINSHIP AND SOCIAL ORGANIZATION

BY

W. H. R. RIVERS

M.D., F.R.S.

Together with 'The Genealogical
Method of Anthropological Enquiry'

*With Commentaries by Raymond Firth and
David M. Schneider*

UNIVERSITY OF LONDON
THE ATHLONE PRESS
NEW YORK: HUMANITIES PRESS INC.
1968

Published by
THE ATHLONE PRESS
UNIVERSITY OF LONDON
at 2 Gower Street, London, WCI
Distributed by Constable & Co Ltd
12 Orange Street, London, WC2

Canada
Oxford University Press
Toronto

485 19534 8

Library of Congress Catalog Card No. 67–17557

PRINTED IN GREAT BRITAIN BY
ROBERT CUNNINGHAM AND SONS LTD
ALVA

CONTENTS

FIGURES

Diagrams in *Kinship and Social Organization*

Introduction

William Halse Rivers Rivers was born in 1864 and died in 1922. More than fifty years have passed since, when a Fellow of St. John's College, Cambridge, he delivered these three lectures on kinship at the London School of Economics and Political Science.[1]

During this half century, in the many generations of British social anthropologists three categories may be distinguished with reference to this work. There are those, like Malinowski (who attended the Lectures), Radcliffe-Brown and Brenda Seligman, who learned directly from Rivers; there are those, like myself and some of my contemporary colleagues, who never knew Rivers but found his influence still fresh when we came to work in London in the nineteen twenties; and there are our students in turn, for many of the most recent of whom Rivers is almost a legend and even Malinowski only a name. Obviously, there has been a great advance in kinship studies since Rivers's time. The ethnography based on kinship inquiry has been vastly widened. About the Trobrianders, the Tikopia, the Samoans and the various Nilotic, Pueblo and other peoples mentioned by Rivers, we now know so much as to make his tentative statements seem crude indeed. (Though for the Banks islands and Santa Cruz it is only very recently that we have had much more scholarly information than Rivers himself collected.)

Progress in kinship ethnography at the present time cannot, of course, be attributed solely or even largely to the influence of

---

[1] Published in 1914 by Constable and Co Ltd, as No. 36 in the Series of Monographs by Writers connected with the School, the series, entitled Studies in Economic and Political Science, was edited by the Hon. W. Pember Reeves, Director of the School. (Malinowski's *Argonauts of the Western Pacific*, published in 1922, was No. 65 in this Series.) One index to the passage of time is seen in the fact that the original edition of Rivers's three lectures was sold as a book of nearly one hundred pages, in a blue cloth cover with gilt lettering, for only 2/6d.

In conformity with modern spelling usage the title in this edition is referred to throughout as *Kinship and Social Organization*. The original had *Organisation*.

Rivers. But efficient collection of kinship data in the field has continued to use as a prime instrument some version of the genealogical method first specifically formulated and advocated by Rivers as a result of his own field research in the Torres Straits and among the Todas. This work is not without blemish. The studies of Emmeneau among the Todas revealed a type of structure which Rivers had not perceived. In his methodological paper Rivers asserts that no knowledge of the vernacular is needed to collect kinship information effectively by the use of genealogies —a claim which few modern anthropologists would be prepared to support. Moreover, apart from modern refinements of the method which have been introduced, genealogical inquiry needs to be supplemented by some form of sociological census in order to yield the best results. Again, while the technique is simple it is very time-consuming if systematically pursued, and raises difficulties of application on a sampling basis for large populations, as Herskovits has indicated. Nevertheless, it is recognized, as Herskovits himself has pointed out (1948, pp. 89–91), that the genealogical method is essentially associated with the name of Rivers and if adequately used 'lays bare a broad range of information concerning the social structures and other institutions of the people being studied'. It has seemed appropriate, then, to reprint a contribution of such historical interest to the field anthropologist.

But if kinship ethnography has expanded greatly since Rivers's day, the climate of opinion, the way of thinking theoretically about kinship, has altered even more. Rivers held as a cardinal assumption in the lectures delivered at the London School of Economics that systems of kinship terminology give a valuable instrument for studying the history of social institutions, especially forms of marriage. This thesis is now outmoded except in some special features. It was already outmoded in fact at the time of its enunciation by Rivers. A. R. Radcliffe-Brown has told us how at that time he disagreed with Rivers and challenged his methodological bias towards conjectural history (1941, repub. 1952, pp. 50–1). B. Malinowski, before the lectures were published, had already issued a book which quietly ignored Rivers's major preoccupation, though it criticized in the work of others the sacrifice of the understanding of actual facts to 'sterile speculation upon a hypothetical earlier state of things'. Malinowski proclaimed there the position which he and practically all later social anthropologists were to take up, and which left much of Rivers's analysis high and dry—the 'first postulate of scientific study: the possibility of an adequate description of facts and their mutual dependences as they exist now in living, primitive societies' (1913, pp. vii, ix).

Why then should it be thought worth while reissuing these London lectures? While the main stream of kinship theory has swung right away from Rivers's position and is not likely ever to return, it is clear that the influence of Rivers on his contemporaries was profound and on his successors has been significant. Malinowski, in the work to which reference has been made, acknowledges his debt to Rivers for the 'constant aid and counsel generously given'. Radcliffe-Brown, while registering his adverse criticism of Rivers's method in the field of historical reconstruction, also records his esteem for Rivers as man, as teacher and as scientist. From the other side of the Atlantic A. L. Kroeber, stigmatizing the massive *History of Melanesian Society* as 'nearly valueless and essentially fantastic as a piece of history', still paid tribute to Rivers as an 'unusually able scientist'.[1] R. H. Lowie, who told Kroeber (Kroeber, 1952, p. 173) that he had been 'immensely stimulated by Rivers's *Kinship and Social Organization*', gave evidence of this when he wrote that, stimulated by Rivers, he tested some of Rivers's views in the light of North American data and found them confirmed (1920, pp. 115, 154). Apart from his psychological and anthropological studies in the Torres Straits and his great volume on the Todas, which remain permanent descriptive contributions, Rivers's work on kinship is still often cited, as by Tax,[2] Murdock and Lévi-Strauss. In his Inaugural lecture as William Wyse Professor of Social Anthropology at Cambridge, Fortes paid homage to the greatness of Rivers, first of the Cambridge social anthropologists. An inaugural lecture is an institutionalized occasion for graceful compliments.

[1] From a lecture delivered in 1938, see Kroeber, 1952, p. 82.

[2] Tax stated 'To most anthropologists today, Rivers is the founder of the modern study of social organization', and credits him with responsibility for the modern theoretical study of cross-cousin marriage systems (1955, pp. 471, 520). Curiously, S. F. Nadel gives citation to the psychological work of Rivers in Index, Bibliography and at least one footnote to 'F. W. H. Rivers'—possibly due to an unconscious association with the work of F. W. H. Myers and of C. S. Myers (companion of Rivers in the Torres Straits), with which he undoubtedly would have been familiar (Nadel, 1951).

Yet Fortes had no hesitation in saying that Rivers's basic hypotheses were absurd—an opinion with which few modern British
social anthropologists would disagree. But he gave to Rivers the
credit of beginning British research in the study of family and
kinship institutions, of being among the first to show that knowledge of a people's social structure is the key to their whole
social life, and even said that there was genius in some of Rivers's
work (Fortes, 1953, pp. 26–7, 40).

In these opinions of his contemporaries and of his successors
about the character of Rivers's work there is clearly a paradox
which we must attempt to resolve.

Independently, David Schneider and I had come to the view
that it was time for a reappraisal of these Lectures on Kinship
and Social Organization, and on learning this Schneider very
generously agreed to allow his commentary to form part of the
present work. It is hoped that our joint contributions may throw
some further light on Rivers's theoretical approach and on the
reasons for the enduring character of his results.

London, June 1966   RAYMOND FIRTH

PART ONE
Commentaries

Rivers and Kroeber in the Study of Kinship

by David M. Schneider

Most of the nineteenth and early twentieth-century anthropological theory was largely devoted to attempts to write the evolution and/or the history of human culture and society. There was an especially keen search for The Origin of things on the assumption that if The Origin could be discovered, this would explain—more or less—the present state of whatever it was that was of interest.

Such questions as whether a stage of polyandry was necessary, whether matrilineal descent preceded patrilineal, whether there ever had been a state of primitive promiscuity, whether group marriage immediately followed exogamy were some of the central concerns.

To deal with such questions, evidence had to be presented. It was not possible simply to assert that a state of primitive promiscuity preceded the division of the earliest society into two out-marrying units, and that exogamy and group marriage came before the development of the elementary family. On analogy with geology, survivals constituted the most persuasive evidence on such questions. A fossil, or the tail on the human embryo, constituted concrete evidence and as such could be respected.

In 1871 L. H. Morgan published *Systems of Consanguinity and Affinity of the Human Family*. In it he presented an extraordinarily ingenious way of reconstructing the early stages of the evolution of man's culture and society. Morgan proposed that patterns of kinship terminology contained the survivals, the concrete evidence for the existence of earlier forms of family organization.

Morgan proceeded on the assumption that social forms determine terminological usages. That is, when kinsmen are classified together it is because they are identical in some important social

7

respect, and when they are classed separately it is because they are different in some important social respect.

Concerned to show that the elementary family, as he knew it in upper New York State and elsewhere in the civilized world, was the most advanced stage in the evolution of familial and social institutions, Morgan divided all terminological systems into two basic types. He called these 'Descriptive' and 'Classificatory'. The distinction between these two types is quite simple and clear. Nowadays we would say that in the Descriptive type, ego's *lineal* relatives are distinguished from his *collateral* relatives. In the Classificatory system, ego's lineal and collateral relatives are terminologically merged. Father is a lineal relative, father's brother a collateral. If father is distinguished from father's brother, then merging does not take place; if father is classed with father's brother then lineal and collateral relatives are merged. But if mother's brother is classed with father's brother, as is the case with the English term 'uncle', although this *classifies* mother's brother with father's brother, it does not classify lineal with collateral relatives, and thus is not the crucial characteristic of what Morgan called the Classificatory system. Morgan seemed well aware of the fact that different relatives were classed together; he was concerned to show that one *kind* of classification, the Descriptive, was a later evolutionary development than another *kind* of classification, the Classificatory.

Why should father be classed with mother's brother in the Classificatory system? The answer, Morgan argued, lay in the fact that systems of kinship terminology are determined by social rules and social institutions. Because they change slowly, earlier forms of social regulation can still be read from them. The reason why the father and mother's brother are classed together in the Classificatory system was quite simple. If a woman married her brother, then a man's father would also be his mother's brother. Father and mother's brother being the same person, it was only reasonable that they should be called by the same kinship term. Where father and mother's brother are called by the same kinship term, therefore, this is a survival of this form of marriage.

Morgan was attacked on many different fronts, but his basic conception that kinship terminologies were the outcome of specific social forms and practices, and his division between Descriptive and Classificatory types, survived most of the attacks. Indeed, Kohler (1897), defending Morgan, discriminated between the Choctaw and Omaha subtypes of the Classificatory system (we call the Choctaw the Crow type now) and argued that the first followed from a specific rule where ego married mother's brother's wife, and the second from the rule which required ego to marry his wife's brother's daughter. Tylor (1889) pointed out that exogamy and the Classificatory system were but two sides of the same fundamental institution, and Durkheim (1898) reviewing Kohler suggested that the Crow–Omaha types were less a consequence of the marriage rules that Kohler postulated than of matrilineal and patrilineal descent rules.

Rivers, too, accepted Morgan's distinction between the Classificatory and Descriptive systems and in 1907 proposed an origin of the Classificatory system which differed from Morgan's but was well within the framework of Morgan's evolutionary theory.

But Rivers's position was to change. W. H. R. Rivers was born in 1864 and trained in medicine. He worked on the physiology of the senses, in experimental psychology and later in psychiatry. He went on the justly famous Cambridge expedition to Torres Straits and, with William McDougall and C. S. Myers, systematically compared the sensory responses of the natives with those of English undergraduates. His ethnographic reports were very useful, and he developed what he called the Genealogical Method for collecting kinship terminology, marriage rules and other social data. Rivers used the Genealogical Method again in his work among the Todas of south India, and later in Melanesia and Polynesia. Rivers's work among the Todas was reported in a monograph in 1906; in 1907 his paper 'On the Origin of the Classificatory System of Relationships' appeared in the Tylor *Festschrift*; in 1908 he went on the Percy Sladen Trust Expedition to Melanesia and Polynesia. Rivers changed his mind by the time he had returned from that trip and begun to analyse and write up his materials; he abandoned evolution and took up diffusion as the major force behind culture change.

But before Rivers's change of mind could be made widely known, A. L. Kroeber, in 1909, launched a sharp, brilliant attack on the idea that either evolutionary or historical reconstructions could safely be made from kinship terms, that any uni-directional,

simple kind of determinism could account for terminological
patterns, and on the idea that the classificatory system had any
significant meaning. The last paragraph in Kroeber's paper throws
down the gauntlet clearly. 'Terms of relationship reflect psychology, not sociology. They are determined primarily by
language and can be utilized for sociological inferences only with
extreme caution.'

Rivers's *History of Melanesian Society* proved to be a two-
volume work, the first of which reported much new ethnographic material. (But see Firth, 1936, pp. xxiii–xxiv for some
critical remarks on this.) The second, a remarkable synthesis,
purports to do just what its title promised. It stated what Rivers
believed to be the History of Melanesian Society reconstructed
largely on the basis of terminological patterns.

If Kroeber's 1909 paper was right, therefore, Rivers's 1914 work
was fruitless. Kroeber could not be ignored. Further, Rivers
needed the opportunity to state his new position simply, clearly,
and forcefully before the *magnum opus* appeared. This brilliant
little book by Rivers entitled *Kinship and Social Organization* was
the result. It appeared early in the same year that the *History of
Melanesian Society* appeared, but it was delivered as a series of
lectures at the London School of Economics and Political Science
the year before.

Rivers ignored Kroeber's attempt to designate the significant
formal criteria or principles out of which kin term systems are
constructed—criteria such as generation, age, sex of speaker, sex
of relative, etc. which have become staples in formal analytic
procedures today. Instead, Rivers stayed very close to his 'X
determines Y' formula that is, social conditions determine kin
term systems, even though it was precisely this formula which
Kroeber attacked. At the same time Rivers mistook Kroeber's
meaning of words like 'language' and 'psychology'.

What each saw as the basic issue was the question of whether
anthropology was to be a science. If it was to be a science, and
Rivers held firmly that it should be, then it must be able to demonstrate causal connections, determinate relationships, and Rivers
was prepared to do just this.

Kroeber argued that the relationships which Rivers put forth
as determinate were inadequate to sustain the general propositions, and that anthropology had no business pretending to be a

science in the very narrow and limited sense in which Rivers used the term. Kroeber was therefore prepared to show that not only were the instances Rivers cited not proven, but that a detailed analysis of a great mass of material showed that there was only the loosest relationship between social and marriage forms and kinship terms. In 1917 Kroeber replied to this book by Rivers with a monograph on *California Kinship Systems*, and in 1922 Gifford presented much more material on behalf of Kroeber's position bearing on the same general problem.

From Rivers's point of view, Kroeber did not cite a single example of psychological cause. From Kroeber's point of view, each example cited by Rivers was hypothetical as a form of historical reconstruction or was only the demonstration of a concomitant condition which was by no means universal, even if it may have turned out to be frequent. It is one thing to show that when a rule of matrilateral cross-cousin marriage obtains, the word for father-in-law and mother's brother is often the same, but it is quite another thing to argue that the one is the cause of the other.

Much turned on Kroeber's use of the word 'psychology'. Rivers was himself a psychologist, trained in medicine, practised in experimental psychology and in the physiology of the senses. To him psychology meant the careful, systematic laboratory testing of biologically grounded responses which he himself had undertaken along with McDougall and Myers in the Torres Straits. For Rivers, psychology was the *science* of psychology.

But for Kroeber, psychology meant something quite different, though related. Kroeber came of a tradition where 'the mental sciences' consisted of all the things which man did and made. The tradition was the one which let Boas, Kroeber's teacher, write a book about primitive culture called *The Mind of Primitive Man*. For nineteenth-century humanists, economics, history, art, literature, and so on were all products of man's mind and therefore constituted in one form or another ways of studying the mind of man. For Kroeber, therefore, 'psychology' had to do with the features of the human mind which gave form and pattern to the different aspects of culture. Different aspects of culture—kin terms and marriage rules—were both equally the products of the same underlying pattern, not cause and effect to each other.

Words are part of language, and language part of culture, and
B

so too, of course, such things as marriage rules and the rules according to which groups are formed, along with the categories into which groups are differentiated or out of which groups are composed. Rivers's theoretical assumption was simple, and naïve in the extreme. It was that the cultural form, the terminological pattern, the kinship term, existed only as a consequence of an actual state of affairs which had first taken place and was then, in some sense, 'confirmed' by a terminological form created for it. Rivers saw the marriage rule as being different from the kinship terms in one important respect. The marriage rules made people marry in certain ways, and when they married then it might well be that mother's brother was also the father-in-law, and therefore being the same person would be called by one name. But the name, the kinship term, had no comparable causal effect on action, but was only a consequence of it.

Rivers never faced the problem of why kinship terms were consequences, and why marriage rules causes, that is, why one cultural symbol was only a consequence, another a cause. The idea that culture patterns only confirm existing practice is naïve in the extreme, but nonetheless prevalent today.

Neither did Rivers ever face the problem which his whole treatment of terminological patterns as survivals should have forced on him. If under conditions X the terminological pattern Y is a consequence, and if the terminological pattern Y can persist beyond the time when conditions X are no longer present, why is it that the new conditions do not immediately cause a new terminological pattern? The answer, of course, is that a given terminological pattern is suitable to more than one particular set of social conditions. Perhaps caused by one, it is nevertheless compatible with others. A given set of symbols can have a number of different meanings not only at one time, but at different times, without significant alteration in the form of the symbol. Hence if terminological patterns are to be interpreted as survivals, there must be some way of showing, in a particular pattern, what *must* have been one particular set of social conditions which it symbolized, and not merely what those conditions *might* have been; why that pattern persisted despite the presence of new conditions and the disappearance of the causal conditions. The fundamental assumption must also be examined—that it is not merely social conditions in general but marriage rules in particular which are the causes or determinants of terminological patterns must be examined with care.

Rivers's view of culture made it a simple consequence, confirming some practices but not others. But he offered no real explanation for how the cultural symbols changed or when and why they changed.

Kroeber's view was much different, and much closer to views prevalent today. In Kroeber's view, terminological patterns, like any other aspect of culture, are both cause and effect. Terminological patterns can be seen to be both the consequences of patterns of existing arrangements, and also the causes or guides in terms of which such existing arrangements take their shape.

Nowadays, one might say, following Kroeber, that a system of kinship terminology is not a single system of names for a single homogeneous universe of meaning, as Rivers assumed. A given kinship term means different things, at the same time, each thing being a part of a different universe of meaning. The English word uncle 'means' father's brother and mother's brother. But it also 'means' something about how an uncle should behave, how an uncle should act. It is not an error of genealogical reckoning when a man calls an elder, respected but friendly man 'uncle'. It is the use of this word with reference to its meaning as the name for a social role, a way of behaving. But it is also used with reference to yet another universe of 'meanings' quite apart from its genealogical meaning. It is a mode of respectful address within the universe of modes of address and salutations (McLennan, 1876). And this by no means exhausts the 'meanings' of the word uncle, nor the different universes of which each of those meanings is a part. But this does, I think, help to explain why an aunt's husband is called uncle in English even though he is not, of course, a blood relative. It should also be clear from this that what we call a 'kinship term' is not only a term for a kinsman. (Schneider, 1965b, and in press.)

It is worth noting in this connection that Rivers's invention and use of what he called 'the genealogical method' (reprinted here) was not only a direct expression of his assumption that kinship terms had one and only one relevant meaning—namely, kin types —but the very success of this instrument reinforced his assumption and gave him confidence in it. For the fact is that one really can collect a genealogy from any people, and by asking simply for the father, mother, brother, sister, son, daughter, husband or wife of each person on it expand that genealogy as far as the informant's memory will carry him. Then one can ask what the informant 'calls' each named relative, being cautious only to filter out such appellations as seem not to be kinship terms. With this information one can then see, for instance, that for the native the own brother and the father's brother's son are both called by the same term. But the fact remains that although it is possible to learn something about the terms for kinsmen with such a device, it is not possible either to define the domain of kinsmen, the universe of kinship, or to come anywhere near learning enough about the meaning of kinship terms to be of much use. Like any instrument, it can be very useful but is hardly enough to rely on by itself, which is what Rivers sometimes did.

Kroeber's view is in certain respects very close to that of Lévi-Strauss. Consider this passage, for example: 'if the issue were primarily the narrower one of the pre-eminence of so-called psychological and so-called social influences on kinship systems, I should still lay more stress on the former influence, because, after all, kinship systems are terminologies, terminologies are classifications, and classifications are reflections of "psychological" processes . . .' (1917, p. 395).

Because kinship terms mean different things, and terminological systems impinge on different universes of meaning, the kinds of almost perfect correlations which could have been expected, if Rivers was correct, have never been possible. This is not because perfect or nearly perfect correlations are unlikely in socio-cultural matters, but only for the usual reasons, namely, that the hypothesis being tested is faulty. If kinship terms were *only* a function of marriage rules, then the correlations should be perfect. They are not. Therefore the correlations such as they are, are weak. Rivers of course explained the discrepancy and exceptions as a consequence of change—the terms survived, the social forms disappeared. But the modern followers of Rivers still argue very much as if terminological patterns only had a single universe of meaning, namely, classification of kinsmen according to forms of social organization, and that forms of social organization cause or determine kinship terminological patterns. Murdock's *Social Structure* is an example of this, and his low or weak correlations are referred to change when of course it is really the fundamental weakness of his hypothesis which the poor correlations demonstrate.

The position Rivers took in this little book prospered, whereas Kroeber's fell quietly into disuse. Kroeber never changed his position—indeed, he should not have since he was fundamentally right. But he did say that his choice of the word 'psychological' was unfortunate, and that 'logical' or 'conceptually patterned' was what was at issue. (1917, p. 388; 1952, pp. 172–3.)

What did not prosper was Rivers's historical reconstructions, but the demise of that part of Rivers's work could not be credited to Kroeber. The abandonment of crude historical reconstruction was very general at that time throughout the anthropological world.

What Rivers showed in this little book, and the measure of his greatness, was that with good, reliable information collected in the field by a skilled worker with some intellectual grasp of the problems, kinship systems were at once more complex than had been fully appreciated, yet fundamentally understandable. His *History of Melanesian Society*, and his systematic Toda ethnography are the first careful field studies of kinship. Rivers's greatness lay in his genius for understanding kinship mechanics, and it has been this which has informed anthropological field work and theory ever since. Rivers worked out much of the detail of the relationship between marriage rules, descent rules, and terminological classes and this has stood us in good stead ever since.

If one reads this book to see how different combinations of marriage rules and descent rules yield different categorizations of kinsmen and does not trouble too much over either the question of historical reconstructions or the question of naïve determinism, one can appreciate the contribution of Rivers to the study of social organization and kinship. Once one's appetite is whetted with this little book, one can go on to *The History of Melanesian Society* to see not only more, but more elegant and more elaborately displayed systems, and one can appreciate more fully the special greatness of Rivers's mind and his grasp of what are wonderfully intricate logical systems.

It is an odd irony, worth a further thought, that in regard to the fundamentals of the nature of culture, the nature of history, causality and determinism, and the meaning of kinship terms, in particular, Kroeber was right and Rivers was wrong. Yet Kroeber never really grasped the mechanics of kinship as Rivers did, nor did he ever concede the degree to which terminology forms a system. Although Kroeber's 1909 paper was the foundation for the analysis of kinship systems in terms of formal components as distinct from social forms, Kroeber made no other significant contribution to this problem. Rivers's demonstration of the terminological correlates of cross-cousin marriage is one of his major achievements and has been a contribution of great significance on which generations of further work have been built. Almost all modern work on kinship has taken this more or less directly into account, and much has been based squarely on it. (Radcliffe-Brown, 1952; Lévi-Strauss, 1949; Eggan, 1955, pp. 520ff.).

D.M.S.

Rivers on Oceanic Kinship

by Raymond Firth

The foundations of kinship study, laid by Morgan and McLennan, continued by Starcke, Seebohm, N. W. Thomas and Rivers, were based upon the recognition of four main sets of problems: the categorization of kin beyond the elementary family, as indicated particularly by kinship terminology; the different kinds of formalized relations between different types of kin, and the linkage of these with specific kin terms; the relation of different forms of marriage to kin terminologies; and the specification of different types of kin units, with consequent variation in marriage forms, functions of kin, and kin terms. Refinement of these issues has preoccupied many writers on kinship, and still does so.

Much of Rivers's early scientific work was devoted to the study of problems of experimental psychology, especially in relation to physiology, and on the Cambridge Anthropological Expedition to Torres Straits in 1898 he made precise observations of lasting value on visual acuity, colour vision, visual space perception and allied topics.[1] But he was increasingly drawn towards the study of anthropological problems in the social field. In particular on the Torres Straits expedition and in his later Toda work (1901–2) Rivers was clearly much impressed by the importance of the study of kinship terms. He was very familiar with Lewis H. Morgan's *Systems of Consanguinity and Affinity of the Human Family* (1871), and indeed was largely responsible for restoring this work to the position of serious theoretical consideration to which it was entitled, after having suffered thirty years or so of relative neglect. But his interest in the study of kinship terms may well have been stimulated as much by his taste for problem-solving and for seeking clarification of obscure issues in science as by his familiarity with Morgan's scholarship.

His work in the Toda field allowed Rivers to distinguish in

---

[1] A careful evaluation of Rivers's contribution is given by Morris Ginsberg (1924).

effect terms of address from terms of reference, and so to rescue
the material from Marshall's view of the 'inexplicable confusion
in Toda ideas as to relationship' (Rivers, 1906, p. 483). He was
much interested in what he termed the duties or functions of kin,
and referred in particular to those instances he observed in connection with Toda funerals (e.g. pp. 347–8, 358–60, 498–501).
Here it is clear that he was intrigued by the problem of why
certain persons performed certain actions—such as plucking leaves
to put into the armlet of a dead woman, or laying a cloth on the
dead body, or standing lamenting at the entrance to the crema-
tion enclosure. He found the answer in the bonds of kinship they
had with the deceased, and was particularly impressed by the role
of the child of a maternal uncle or paternal aunt. He found that
infant marriage was common, and that when a man wished to
arrange a marriage for his son he chose a suitable girl 'who should
be, and very often is, the *matchuni* of the boy, the daughter of his
mother's brother or of his father's sister' (p. 502). Since such a
cross-cousin was 'the natural bridegroom or bride' his or her
various kin duties were 'the secondary result' of the marriage
regulation (p. 499). Rivers was also struck by the relation between
the kinship terminology and the form of marriage, and pointed
out that one of the most characteristic features of the Toda
system was the use of the same term for mother's brother and
father-in-law, and for father's sister and mother-in-law (p. 494).

Here in his early field work are the essential ingredients—
special functions of kin, special form of marriage between kin,
special correspondence between consanguineal and affinal kin
terms—which were to appear in much of his later treatment of
kinship. On his return from the Percy Sladen Trust Expedition to
the Solomon islands some years later he pointed out that from his
early work he had reached the belief that in systems of 'relationship' we have, like fossils, the hidden indications of ancient social
institutions. So the stage was set not only for the interpretation of
the present, as was done from the Toda material, but also for the
interpretation of the past from the present.[1] Rivers admitted the
danger of going into the field with such a dominant belief. But

[1] The theme of primitive basis overlain by borrowed traits appeared in various
contexts in Rivers's writings, including some of his psychological work (cf. his
interpretation of massage in Melanesia in a paper read at the 17th International
Congress of Medicine in London in August 1913).

he thought he had guarded himself against this. He held 'that systems of relationship are bodies of dry fact the accuracy of which, especially when collected by the genealogical method (see below, p. 97) is about as incapable of being influenced by bias, conscious or unconscious, as any subject that can be imagined' (1914b, vol. I, pp. 3–4). Yet granted that, as Rivers himself stresses, the linguistic aspects of the situation of collection are adequate, and granted also that no bias has entered into the choice of *which* kinship terms have been collected, there is still the great question of what these 'bodies of dry fact' really mean in their principles of arrangement and in their social context. In my opinion Rivers never squarely faced this question.

One reason, I think, lay in his earlier Toda experiences, which had conditioned him to look for prescribed or preferred marriage forms as associated with usages in classificatory kinship terminology. But I think that another, possibly deeper reason lay in his temperamental approach to the problems of scientific inquiry. I never knew Rivers, having arrived in London two years after he died. But my impression, from Malinowski, Radcliffe-Brown, Brenda Seligman, Bartlett and others, is of a brilliant man, an attractive talker on intellectual topics, fired by ideas almost to a point of becoming obsessed by any one which occupied him at the time, vivid, impressive and charming to students, but basically shy in personal relations and perhaps somewhat remote, even unrealistic, in worldly affairs. This impression[1] is borne out to some extent by his own references to his habits of thought. He wrote in his perceptive work *Conflict and Dream*, of his absorption in his work and his belief in its significance; of his habit, as soon as he was aware that he was awake, of finding that he was thinking over some problem, usually in connection with the scientific work on which he was at the time engaged. He revealed in various ways what he regarded as the intensely scientific character of his mind. He told how he awoke to the sound of an air raid (in the first World War) and then fell asleep again, dreamed of bomb danger and was reproaching himself for showing fear in an air raid, when he realized it was only a dream. He became at once extremely

[1] I am much indebted to Sir Frederick Bartlett, once a pupil of Rivers, for discussing these impressions with me and giving me further information about Rivers's work and personality. I am also grateful to my colleague Dr J. R. Fox for helpful general comment upon this essay.

interested in the experience through which he had passed. 'The occurrence of fear in sleep became at once, on awakening, an object of scientific interest, and this interest removed at once all danger of repression . . .' He then went to sleep again, and slept through the rest of the air raid without wakening! (2nd ed., 1932, pp. 56, 110, 141–2). Rivers drew attention to the striking difference between his dream personality and that of his waking life: in his dreams he was a visualizer, with very definite auditory imagery, whereas in his ordinary life 'I rarely experience imagery, and then usually in so fugitive and vague a form that if my attention had not been attracted to the subject through my scientific interests, I should doubtless never have noticed such capacity for imagery as I possess' (*ibid.*, pp. 94–5). He referred as well to his distrust of analogies. Yet he also held that a desire for change and novelty was one of the strongest elements in his mental make-up (*ibid.*, pp. 85, 134). (Hence perhaps his conversion from evolutionary to 'historical' method.) Rivers was a very complex person, much more emotional than appeared on the surface. His experiences during the war, including his therapeutic work with 'shell-shocked' soldiers, seem to have done much to free him from some inhibitions, and his relations with people at large became much more open. But it would be a fair assumption, it seems to me, that his thinking about scientific matters, while intellectually rigorous within his chosen framework, owed more to deep emotional elements in the choice of this framework than he himself recognized.

All this, as I see it, is relevant to an understanding of how Rivers, with all his analytical skill and power of theoretical construction, could remain so unperceptive of the crudity of his own formulations in the field of kinship terms and marriage relations.

W. H. R. Rivers, more than any other writer of his time, was responsible for sharpening the criteria involved[1] and for putting forward hypotheses about major relationships in the kinship field. His construction of more than one 'definitely outlined scheme' (1907, p. 319)—what in modern language would be called a 'model'—based on clearly stated assumptions, spurred on other anthropologists such as Kroeber, Malinowski, Radcliffe-

[1] Cf. his article 'Kin, Kinship' (1914c) in Hastings' *Encyclopedia of Religion and Ethics*.

Brown, to emulate him or prove the inadequacy of his formulations. But partly as a result of Rivers's own concentration on kinship studies, both the theory of the subject and the character of the ethnographic evidence available have been much amplified and refined in the half-century since his day. This has not reduced argument about the basic issues, but it has become more sophisticated.

As an example, controversy has recently arisen about the very basic concept of the study—the kind of categorization implied by what are conventionally described as 'kinship' terms. Do they, as is popularly supposed, represent relationships which can be thought of as primarily genealogical with an ultimate 'ideal' referent of a biological character? Or do they represent a specific idiom of social relationship in which the biological component is minimal and ultimately irrelevant?[1] Rivers, who was very familiar with the notion that the term 'father' could be applied to a mother's sister's husband, might well have enjoyed the idea of discriminating between 'father' as 'pater', as 'genitor' and as 'genetic father'. But with all his ingenuity, he did not get so far; to him, these 'bodies of dry fact' had an obvious biological referent.

Where the difference between Rivers's view and the modern views appears most markedly is in the concept of marriage. Rivers did a very great service to the study of kinship and to the development of social anthropology generally in stressing with great clarity—if at times on wrong assumptions—the notion that marriage was not a simple personal choice but a category arrangement—a relation between specified types of kin. For him 'forms of marriage' meant not different types of ceremony uniting two people but different types of kin position represented by the two people united—cross-cousins, man and brother's daughter, man and mother's brother's wife, etc. No type of kin union was too bizarre to allow him to refuse it theoretical validity. More than any other anthropologist of his generation, he paved the way for modern structural analyses of kinship in this field.

But his treatment of the content of marriage was naïve. Rivers remained all his life a bachelor, and his view of what marriage involved, at least as implied in his writings, was an extraordinarily limited one. He regarded it as an 'institution', basic to social

[1] See E. Gellner, 1957, 1960, 1963; Barnes, 1961; Beattie, 1964; Schneider, 1964, 1965a.

organization,[1] and was aware of the rights and duties pertaining
to spouses, and of the intricate social relationships involved in the
bringing up of their children. But in his use of the concept of
marriage in his theoretical constructions he focused almost entirely on its legalization of sex relations. Much of his treatment in
this volume is taken up with arguing that kin terms are indicative
of past or present habitual marriage rules, but the only context in
which he discusses marriage rule is that of sexual access to women.
So the special feature of Melanesian nomenclature according to
which terms of relationship vary with the sex of the speaker is
treated as the outcome of a change from sexual communism to a
condition in which sexual relations were restricted to the partners
of a marriage. The term which a man uses for his wife's sister
leads back to a social condition arising out of the regulation
of marriage and sexual relations. Rivers rejected the notion
put forward by Morgan, that sexual promiscuity can ever have
been the ruling principle of a people at any stage. But he accepted
the idea that 'group-marriage', or as he preferred to style it,
'organized sexual communism' was prevalent not only in
Melanesia but may have been a feature of the social development
of mankind. All this does not seem to have been so much a preoccupation with sex as such—as an unkind modern critic might
suggest—as a too cerebral and narrow view of what marriage was
about. In this book at least he ignores completely what may be
called the 'considerations' for marriage—the consequential pay-
ments, exchanges of services, assumption of obligations, acquisition of status—which all go to make up the institution in its full
social reality. He focuses on marriage as the transfer of women,
and against his treatment can be levelled with greater force the
charge sometimes laid against Lévi-Strauss of undervaluing the
effect of these 'considerations' upon the actual form and frequency
of marriage.[2] If Rivers had been studying the implications for
kin terminology and other social phenomena of types of marriages
empirically observed then he could have afforded to neglect these
economic and political factors. But for the most part he was
inferring marriage types from kin terminologies alone, and the

[1] Cf. his article on Marriage (1915) where he pointed out that marriage has two
main functions: a means of regulating relations between the sexes, and a means of
determining the relation of a child to the community.
[2] Leach, 1961, pp. 88–90; J. P. B. de Josselin de Jong, 1952, p. 57.

evidence of transfers of goods, services and changes of status should also have been considered to see if they offered any support to his hypotheses. If Rivers had followed up the clue provided by N. W. Thomas,[1] who in this respect anticipated a modern view, he might have produced more plausible hypotheses. Thomas argued that 'terms of relationship' were expressive simply of duties and status and not of more personal 'descriptive' ties. In effect he was arguing, e.g. that the classificatory term translated as 'mother' stood for a 'mothering' relationship, and that the term regarded as connoting 'marital relation' meant not the *existence* of such relation but only spouse *potentiality*. What is important he held in the first case is not the genetic relation between mother and son, but the fact that they belong to different generations; in the second case the point selected for emphasis is the *legality* of marital relations, where existent or not. Rivers was so anxious to prove that marriage, i.e. sex relation, between apparently bizarre kinds of kin was in conformity with social principle, that he overlooked the more significant element of status relation.

These comments can be illustrated from a brief review of Rivers's ideas on four types of marriage or sex union described in this book, in the light of modern findings, particularly from the Oceanic area. These forms of relationship are: with the wife's sister; with the mother's brother's widow; with the cross-cousin; and with the granddaughter or grandmother. (The diagrams I give for illustration follow a different style of presentation from those of Rivers.)

How may the classing of sister-in-law with sister or of brother-in-law with brother be interpreted? Rivers points out that in most of the Melanesian cases (it is true also of Tikopia) a man calls his wife's sister by a sibling term. But it is not the term which he himself uses for his sister, but the same term as his wife uses for hers. Rivers's inference is that the use of this term is intended to be a barrier to sexual intercourse between brother-in-law and sister-in-law. For a man to use his wife's own 'sister' term for this woman means that she is definitely put out of the 'wife' category for him. But Rivers argued, on 'definite evidence' that sexual relations with a wife's sister were formerly allowed, were 'orthodox'. In time, however, they were looked upon as improper, and

[1] N. W. Thomas, 1906, pp. 123–6.

to mark this change a man came to use for his wife's sister the term which he picked up from his wife (1914a, pp. 62–3; cf. 1914b, vol. I, pp. 33–4, 45). But modern social anthropologists see a simpler correlation. A wife's sister is called by 'sibling of same sex' term by a husband. This does not indicate any barrier against sex relations; on the contrary, in Tikopia traditionally it was with his wife's sister that a man not infrequently contracted a polygynous marriage (Firth, 1936, p. 566). What the use of 'sibling of the same sex' and not 'sibling of different sex' indicates primarily in such a society is that the man is not bound to render to his wife's sister and her children similar obligations as he is bound to render to a woman whom he calls his 'sibling of opposite sex', in other words, his own sister (Firth, 1958, pp. 4–5). Rivers's preoccupation with the theme of sex relations alone and in the reconstructed past at that, inhibited him from seeing just how, as he himself said in this context, the terminology of relationship here indeed 'reflects' sociology. If he had paid more attention to what he himself described elsewhere as the 'functions of kin' implied by these terms, he might have seen this reflection more adequately. It is interesting to note that Rivers himself was critical of Morgan at one point below pp. 41–2) for his zeal in reconstructing a past situation to provide a basis for kin terminology.

Rivers was the first to demonstrate fully the kin term implications of cross-cousin marriage, with the equation of mother's brother and father-in-law, etc., and the consequent merging of the appropriate kin terms. From this method of looking at marriage as a manipulation of relationships in category terms has come a vast development of rigorous analytical propositions. This is a critical case for the whole development of his theory, and the line of his argument should be carefully followed.

In the first Lecture, after a generalized example of bilateral cross-cousin union, 'as is usual', he instances the Mbau system of Fiji, where 'we know' the cross-cousin marriage to be an established institution, and the terminology can be regarded as 'the direct and inevitable consequence' of it. Similarly he argues for the Southern New Hebrides. But for Guadalcanal the argument slides round. The same term (*nia*) is used for mother's brother and wife's father; with FZH and husband's father it was *probable* alsost but not eablished by evidence.[1] Still it appeared to Rivers that there 'seemed to be no doubt' that it was the custom for a man to marry his MBD or FZD, even though he was not able to demonstrate this form of marriage genealogically. Nevertheless, he included Guadalcanal as one of the only parts of Melanesia where he 'found' the practice of the cross-cousin marriage. He went on to ask 'If it were not for the cross-cousin marriage, what can there be to give the mother's brother a greater psychological similarity to the father-in-law than the father's brother . . .?'

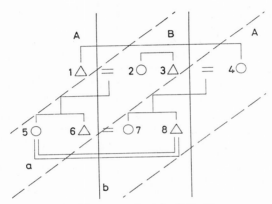

FIG. I. 'Correspondence' of Kin Terms

If he had been more in sympathy with the approach of, say, Tylor or N. W. Thomas, the answer might have been 'an exo-gamous dual organization'. As Rivers himself noted elsewhere (1914b, vol. I, pp. 17–18), this could allow mother's brother, father's sister's husband and wife's father, all men of similar status and same senior generation, to be regarded as in the same category. In a patrilineal moiety system they would all be members of the opposite moiety to his own; in a matrilineal system, more common in Melanesia, they would all be members of his own moiety. Of course, if reciprocal cross-cousin marriage did take place, they

---

[1] In this Lecture Rivers states that his stay in Guadalcanal was not long enough to enable him to collect sufficient genealogical material to demonstrate these points completely. But in the *History of Melanesian Society* (1914b, vol. I, p. 244) he states only that it is *possible* that the term is also used for the husband of the father's sister. There is a subtle difference! (These kin terms were obtained from a single informant during 'a hasty visit' to the north-west of the island.)

would all be the same man. (Rivers noted this point as a complication, but set it aside (below, p. 53).)

With reciprocal cross-cousin marriage, man 6 marries woman 7, and 3 is consequently his mother's brother, wife's father and father's sister's husband. If the moiety system is matrilineal, 6 and 3 are in the same moiety (a); if patrilineal, in opposite moieties (A and B).

But the Guadalcanal system is not that of a dual organization; as Rivers himself found, it comprises six matrilineal exogamous clans. Without postulating any regular marriage arrangements between pairs of clans the alignment of mother's brother with wife's father and father's sister's husband can be fairly simply explained on the principle of economy of classification. In this matrilineal exogamous system the important thing is to distinguish primarily between those who are or may be of my own group and those who must be of another. My mother must be distinguished from my father's sister and my wife's mother; my mother's brother from my mother's husband, i.e. my father. In any system which is economical of kin terms it is simple to have one term, e.g. *nia* for all males senior to me by a generation who are in my group, and another, *mama* for all those who are not. Now my wife's father may or may not be of my father's group, but my father's sister's husband definitely cannot be of this group. Both conceivably may be of my own group. Hence in operating with a small budget of terms it makes good sense to have these last two men in my *nia* category rather than in my *mama* category. The occurrence of cross-cousin marriage would strengthen this rationale but is not required by it. But what is of major significance in this example is that the terms *nia* and *mama* indicate not specific genealogical relationships, but categories of relationships, and this destroys the simple, precise identification of marriage partners in the manner Rivers postulated.

But already Rivers had reached the point of correlating kin term equivalences with *antecedent* marriage conditions for which there was no independent contemporary evidence.

In the second Lecture he begins with a Banks Islands exemplar of the now well-known Crow type usage of a person calling his FZS by the same term as his father. He looks for a 'social custom' which can give meaning to this usage, and finds it in marriage with mother's brother's wife or widow. This illustrates his myopia very well. He has seen rightly that the equivalence of terms indicates some kind of equation between a mother's brother and a sister's son. He has seen also that it is an equation in respect of some form of rights and obligations. Furthermore, he has recognized that this equation involves consequential adjustment in the position of other members of the kin circle, so that the mother's brother's children become the 'children' of the man concerned. But the only rights and obligations Rivers can suggest are those of marriage. Yet a little reflection might have indicated a firmer basis for his linkage of kin terms with social conditions. Marriage with mother's brother's widow is a personal act, depending on a double availability, and Rivers has noted that in the Banks Islands it seems to have been an obligation only if the deceased husband had a nephew *who was not yet married*. In other words, the phenomenon may well have been a discontinuous one (if indeed it really was ever common). But in the fields of property rights, exercise of authority, and general status accorded by the social rules, a sister's son could be *always* equivalent to his mother's brother. Even in childhood a father's sister's son could demand from his cross-cousins the tokens of respect equivalent to those paid to their father. From another viewpoint he 'ascends into his mother's place' as Codrington put it (1891, p. 39; cf. Rivers, 1914b, vol. I, pp. 33–4, 48).

In this field modern research has unequivocally thrown up a great mass of evidence for the inadequacy of Rivers's reconstruction, and the validity of the broader formulation. This has the added merit of being intelligible—and observable—in contemporary conditions. In the Melanesian field one of the best early demonstrations of this was given by R. F. Fortune in his work on Dobu (1932, pp. 38, 40). There the FZS is called 'father', but only after the death of his mother's brother; till then he is called by a term which may be rendered as 'cross-cousin'. When his mother's brother dies he is not expected to marry the widow, but he is expected to inherit the status and property of the mother's brother, and to have the authority over the children which their father formerly had. So it is quite logical that he should be called 'father', not 'cousin' when their father dies. The effect is an 'elevation of the inheriting group'.

In his analysis of the implications of cross-cousin marriage Rivers hardly concerned himself at all with the major group

C

relations involved. It is in this sphere above all that modern kinship study, while following in his initial track, has made a major and largely independent contribution. Rivers barely differentiated for purposes of exposition, between matrilateral and patrilateral cross-cousin marriage, and seems to have thought that they were normally alternatives in the same society. The many analytical contributions in this field, highlighted by the work of Radcliffe-Brown, Lévi-Strauss, Leach, Schneider, Needham—to mention only a few—have revealed the fundamental sociological significance of variations in practice here, especially when linked with different rules of descent, status and reciprocity. Simple diagrams illustrating a few of these variations will show how far the

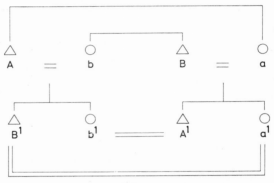

FIG. 2. Reciprocal Cross-cousin Marriage

exemplars given by Rivers must be revised in order to give a more sensitive and more adequate picture of the meaning of cross-cousin marriage.

In this marriage, with exchange of sisters, a man marries a woman who is both his MBD and his FZD. In each generation then the result is a continual involution of the two descent groups concerned. Theoretically, with no wider contacts, the two groups may be expected to exchange not only women but also many kinds of other goods and services. Their integration should be very high, but their possibilities of integration with other units of the wider society correspondingly reduced. The 'Kariera type' of marriage structure described by Radcliffe-Brown is one variety of this system. Hence the whole system has been labelled by Lévi-Strauss 'restricted exchange', and the implications for limited social cohesion drawn by him with great refinement.

If marriage with FZD occurs alone as the pattern, with union with MBD barred, then there is still an interchange of women between two groups, but in *alternate* generations.

In such a system a man's sister's daughter marries his son and his daughter's daughter marries his son's son. His father's father and his MMB are the same person. His mother's brother cannot be his father-in-law since MBD union is prohibited. To provide his wife's father a member of a third group is required. If the

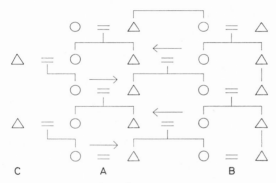

FIG. 3. Patrilateral Cross-cousin Marriage

system is one of patrilineal descent groups then a man and his son are of the same group, but the son's wife is of a different group than that of her father-in-law. The reverse is the case in a matrilineal system such as the Trobriands. If such a marriage takes place, the young man marrying takes his wife from his father's descent group while he himself belongs to his mother's brother's group. In the Trobriands Malinowski has pointed out that a brother may take the initiative in asking his sister for her daughter in marriage for his son. A contract of infant betrothal is confirmed by exchanges of food. Malinowski regarded such cross-cousin marriage as a compromise 'between the two ill-adjusted principles of mother right and father love'. But it is clear from subsequent analysis by other writers that structural principles rather than personal sentiment are responsible. On the other hand, structure and sentiment may be closely interwoven, as when one of Malinowski's Trobriand friends explained that he wanted his little son to marry his sister's daughter because he wanted a daughter-in-law who would be a real kinswoman. When he was old he would then have someone of his own kin group to look after him, cook his food, bring him his lime pot and lime stick, and pull out his grey hairs, without having to fear sorcery (1932, p. 87).

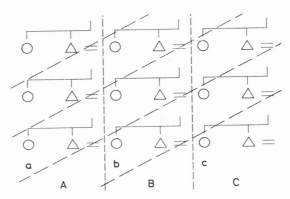

FIG. 4a. Matrilateral Cross-cousin Marriage in genealogical terms

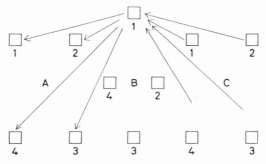

FIG. 4b. Matrilateral Cross-cousin Marriage in sub-group terms

When we look at a third type of cross-cousin marriage, MBD but with FZD prohibited, a different pattern of group relation is apparent. The implications of this type of structural arrangement have been elaborately investigated by E. R. Leach in 1951 (1961, pp. 54–104). In this case the transfer of women in marriage is always one way (Fig. 4a). One group gives its daughters continually to the men of another, but there is no reciprocity in women. The men of this group must by rule hand on their sisters and daughters to other groups. The asymmetrical character of these marriage alliances tends to promote reciprocity in goods and services, and many of the societies which practise this form of marriage regularly use the marriage contributions as status indicators.

If the structure is one of matrilineal descent groups mother's brother and sister's son get wives from the same group and father and son from different groups. If the structure is one of patrilineal descent groups, father and son get wives from the same group, but while a man as sister's son gets a wife from his mother's brother's group, a mother's brother's wife must come from still another group. This system demands then a series of groups involved in unilateral transfer of women in marriage. If a theoretical model, with very limited possibilities, be envisaged such that each group gives women to only one other group, then a system of what has been termed circulating connubium can obtain.[1] But, *de facto*, the strength of lineage or local group organization is such that each such group normally gives wives to more than one other group and the system is therefore more complex. Moreover, marriages of this type, like many others between persons identified by kinship categories, are commonly not between the closest kin of these designations but between classificatory kin. There is therefore considerable flexibility in choice of marriage partners and in taking into consideration economic and political circumstances related to the marriage. Leach (1961, pp. 81–90) has been able to show very effectively how the matrilateral cross-cousin marriage system of the Kachin, despite its seeming asymmetry, is in fact on the whole in political and economic balance. The resultant of such a system of asymmetrical wife-giving and reciprocal exchanges in other goods is to maintain an intricate system of interlocking relationships between the different groups in the society, so that Lévi-Strauss has been able to designate this system as one of 'generalized exchange'.

It is clear from such evidence that the type of marriage and the type of kin terminology are likely to be closely related. But they would seem to be related not causally in a temporal sequence but through their dependence on the group structure of the society and the kinds of mechanisms customarily used to validate group

[1] Cf. Leach, 1961, pp. 55, 73; Needham, 1962, p. 7.

interest and notions of group status, as well as the immediate concerns of individuals.

It is important to realize that a custom such as 'matrilateral cross-cousin' marriage if it can be identified as of regular operation, is essentially conceived as a category transaction, not a genealogical union. It is a structural arrangement between groups, asymmetrical as regards the passage of women but compensated for by the reverse passage of goods or services or maintenance/ acquisition of status. And with the diversification involved by the linkage of any one group with a number of others, as Leach has indicated, the likelihood of a man getting as his bride a daughter of his mother's own brother is small indeed and of no particular significance to the structure of the system as a whole. Thus if for the genealogical diagram in Figure 4a be substituted sets of local lines, say four in each of the three major groups A, B, and C, the central group B would be involved in receiving women from C along sixteen channels and giving women to A along sixteen other channels (Fig. 4b shows the effect on only one of the four local units of B). It is then as symbols of affinity rather than as mother's brother's daughters that the transfer of women is effected, and the kin category terminology is in accord with this.

Each society has its own methods of facilitating co-operation and integration and the various forms of preferred cross-cousin marriage assist in these in various ways. Rivers writes 'I do not suppose that, even in this subject, there will be found anyone to claim that the Fijians took to marrying their cross-cousins because such a marriage was suggested to them by the nature of their system of relationship' (p. 53). He is writing here of the *nomenclature* of relationship only. But if one understands by system of relationship not just a system of kin terms but the general mode of kin behaviour, including the exercise of property rights, then modern anthropology does indeed suppose that 'cross-cousin' marriage is one of the possible correlates, if not a consequence.

What Rivers himself described as a marriage of apparently most bizarre and complex character also arises from his consideration of Melanesian evidence, particularly from the island of Raga (Pentecost) and the Trobriands. In both areas he inferred marriage with a daughter's daughter or with a granddaughter of a brother (1914a, pp. 35–6; 1914b, vol. I, pp. 198–204; vol. II, pp. 47–8, 56–69). Marriage with a relative two generations apart may seem to us ludicrous. But evidence from Australia shows clearly that the whole system of control of rights in women does allow, in the traditional system, marital unions between elderly men and young girls. Odd and even repugnant as such a custom might seem to be to us, then, it cannot necessarily be ruled out. But it should be noted that even in Australia such a marriage between persons of disparate generations was not the rule but only one of the implications of the structure of the system. Even in Australia it could not be maintained that the regularity of such a type of marriage resulted in an equation of terminology between granddaughter and wife or analogous relative. The major clue which could have helped to explain the apparent anomalies in kinship terminology, namely the equivalent status given to persons of alternate generations, was one which Rivers rejected (p. 61). Rivers finds that his record of Raga kin terms corresponds exactly with the daughter's daughter marriage he had inferred. Yet if the terms which he cites be set out in the form of relationships between members of exogamous matrilineal moieties, the system is quite comprehensible if a man marries his first cousin, i.e. his mother's brother's daughter instead of his daughter's daughter (Fig. 5). In this case, as in most of the others adduced by Rivers, the equation of kinship terms is a *status* equation, not a marriage equation.[1]

The situation is illustrated most clearly by the material from the Trobriands which Rivers regarded as supported by other Melanesian usages to indicate marriage with a daughter's daughter. He infers this from the fact that the term *tabu* is applied both to grandparents and to father's sister's child (p. 72).

The literature of Trobriand kinship, including the use of the term *tabu*, is now quite extensive, and various usages mentioned by Malinowski have been shown to fit intelligible structural alignments.[2] Fortes (1957, p. 176) showed for example that the term for FZS recorded by Malinowski as an anomalous linguistic extension of the term for 'father', conforms to the general type of situation in which a matrilineal male heir is recognized as the father's successor (see above, p. 27). He and other writers have with some justice

[1] This question is discussed from the same point of view by Ginsberg 1924, p. 42, who refers to Lowie's similar criticism.
[2] Marguerite Robinson, 1962; cf. Leach, 1958; Powell, 1960; Julius, 1960; Fathauer, 1961; Uberoi, 1962; Marie Reay, 1963; Lounsbury, 1965; Sider, 1967.

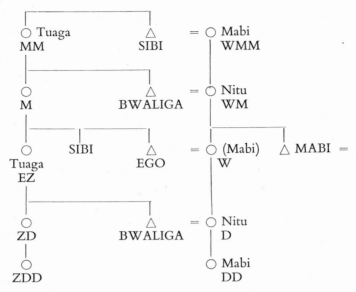

FIG. 5. Raga Kin Terms according to Rivers (below, p. 60).

pointed out that Malinowski confused indices of a jural order in the society with those showing up individual motive and sentiment.

The term *tabu*, which is critical in Rivers's argument, was described by Malinowski in a series of graded terms with functional definition. According to him it has a 'primary' meaning of father's sister, but also embraces FZD and paternal cross-cousin more generally. 'By extension' it includes all women of the father's clan and even in its widest sense all women not of the same clan. But in its most extensive application it means lawful woman, the woman with whom intercourse is possible as distinct from a matrilineal kinswoman with whom intercourse is barred (1932, pp. 88, 180, 423, 450–51). A man's *tabu* perform an important role for him. They are approved suitable partners for passing intrigues and for more stable liaisons. When beauty magic is to be performed, each boy before washing leaves his most precious ornaments with his *tabu*. Later they stroke him with these and recite formulae to improve his skin and looks. When a woman is pregnant it is her *tabu* who make her marriage robe, who wash her, decorate her, and so on (pp. 180, 185, 292, 296, 298). What is quite clear from Malinowski's account is that Rivers was completely mistaken in identifying *tabu* simply with granddaughter and grandparent. It does mean both grandparent and MMB as well as grandchild (Powell, 1960, Malinowski, 1932, p. 449). But the term applies equally to FZD and much more generally to women in the father's clan. Hence, given the Trobriand patrilateral cross-cousin preference—even though it operates in practice not very frequently—for a man to marry a *tabu* would be not a 'peculiar and exceptional feature' (below, p. 72).[1]

What has been said above, however, does not completely dispose of the problem of what a *tabu* is. Leach in particular has devoted considerable attention to this question in an article on the subject (1958). He argues in effect that the category of *tabu* refers really to marginal relatives and is not only vague but ambiguous. He minimizes the incidence of patrilateral cross-cousin marriage, saying that it is rare and largely confined to the families of chiefs, and distinguishes *tabu* as all those who are not involved in the complex transactions of food presentation known by the Trobrianders as *urigubu*. Since in the long run the sons of a man's sisters will inherit his gardens, his sons look upon their cross-cousins as usurpers. Though in one sense according to Malinowski they are in the category of friends, they are friends who bode no good. Hence, argues Leach, the term *tabu* applied to a father's sister and kin of the same general category is the same as the term *tabu* meaning prohibited or forbidden. (This is in flat opposition to Malinowski, who argues that the latter is a different word introduced by Christian missionaries as an alternative to the word *boma* which the Trobrianders themselves traditionally used.)

Ingenious as Leach's explanation is, it still leaves certain questions open. It is the father's sisters and their daughters who are the primary *tabu*. The FZSs, the inheritors of the property, are called *tama*, father, which in Trobriand terms is on the whole a label of affection. Moreover, the female *tabu* perform many acts of friendship for a boy. Again *tabu* applies both to grandparents and to MMB, where hostility does not really fit as a label for the relationship. Moreover, if *tabu* is both kin term and taboo, it is odd that the *tabu* term should apply to the kin whom one may marry, whereas the kin to whom the strictest sexual taboo applies

---

[1] Note that Malinowski could find no evidence at all of *marriage* with father's sister.

are not *tabu* but *luta*—an antithetical category! Leach points out too (1958, p. 145) that on marriage a woman, and her immediate kin, 'forthwith cease to be *tabu*'. But it is at this point that a man's brother finds that his brother's wife comes to be *taboo* sexually to him. In other words, *tabu* are not taboo before marriage, but become so (to other close matrilineal kin of the husband) after marriage!

From consideration of all this material in the Oceanic field it is clear that Rivers's proposition about the origination of 'correspondences' in kinship term from 'anomalous' marriages (especially from such marriages in times past) cannot be sustained. Rivers, of course, suffered from a relatively short space of time for his field research in any one area, and complete ignorance of any vernacular language. He therefore was unable by his own efforts to amplify or correct the hints which he thought he had received about marriage arrangements. If he had had the advantage of the material from modern field experience his generalizations would surely have taken another form. He might well have led the way in identifying kin terminologies and their associated 'functions' as total phenomena, semantic systems of verbal and non-verbal behaviour, rather than collections of isolated usages of retrospective import.

What we owe to Rivers above all is the direction of our thinking specifically on the issues of the relation between categories of kin terminology and forms of marriage. In some cases this has resulted in drawing our attention to practices not hitherto recorded (see Tax, 1935, pp. 520–1, 550). Through our scepticism about his generalizations in the form which he presented them we have been led to explore further into the institutional context. The resulting richness of documentation in this whole field owes a great deal to the initial stimulus of Rivers.

R.F.

PART TWO

Kinship and Social Organization

by W. H. R. Rivers

PREFACE

These lectures were delivered at the London School of Economics in May of the present year. They are largely based on experience gained in the work of the Percy Sladen Trust Expedition to Melanesia of 1908, and give a simplified record of social conditions which will be described in detail in the full account of the work of that expedition.

A few small additions and modifications have been made since the lectures were given, some of these being due to suggestions made by Professor Westermarck and Dr Malinowski in the discussions which followed the lectures. I am also indebted to Miss B. Freire-Marreco for allowing me to refer to unpublished material collected during her recent work among the Pueblo Indians of North America.

St. John's College,   W.H.R.R.
Cambridge
19 *November*, 1913

Editorial Note. The spelling of tribes, islands, and countries has been brought into line with current practice.

Lecture I

The aim of these lectures is to demonstrate the close connection which exists between methods of denoting relationship or kinship and forms of social organization, including those based on different varieties of the institution of marriage. In other words, my aim will be to show that the terminology of relationship has been rigorously determined by social conditions and that, if this position has been established and accepted, systems of relationship furnish us with a most valuable instrument in studying the history of social institutions.

In the controversy of the present and of recent times, it is the special mode of denoting relationship known as the classificatory system which has formed the chief subject of discussion. It is in connection with this system that there have arisen the various vexed questions which have so excited the interest—I might almost say the passions—of sociologists during the last quarter of a century.

I am afraid it would be dangerous to assume your familiarity with this system, and I must therefore begin with a brief description of its main characters. The essential feature of the classificatory system, that to which it owes its name, is the application of its terms, not to single individual persons, but to classes of relatives which may often be very large. Objections have been made to the use of the term 'classificatory' on the ground that our own terms of relationship also apply to classes of persons; the term 'brother', for instance, to all the male children of the same father and mother, the term 'uncle' to all the brothers of the father and the mother as well as to the husband of an aunt, while the term 'cousin' may denote a still larger class. It is, of course, true that many of our own terms of relationship apply to classes of persons, but in the systems to which the word 'classificatory' is usually applied, the classificatory principle applies far more widely, and in some cases even, more logically and consistently. In the most complete form of the classificatory system there is not one single term of relationship the use of which tells us that reference is being made to one person and to one person only, whereas in our own system there are six such terms, viz., husband, wife, father, mother, father-in-law and mother-in-law. In those systems in which the classificatory principle is carried to its extreme degree every term is applied to a class of persons. The term 'father', for instance, is applied to all those whom the father would call brother, and to all the husbands of those whom the mother calls sister, both brother and sister being used in a far wider sense than among ourselves. In some forms of the classificatory system the term 'father' is also used for all those whom the mother would call brother, and for all the husbands of those whom the father would call sister, and in other systems the application of the term may be still more extensive. Similarly, the term used for the wife may be applied to all those whom the wife would call sister and to the wives of all those whom the speaker calls brother, brother and sister again being used in a far wider sense than in our own language.

The classificatory system has many other features which mark it off more or less sharply from our own mode of denoting relationship, but I do not think it would be profitable to attempt a full description at this stage of our inquiry. As I have said, the object of these lectures is to show how the various features of the classificatory system have arisen out of, and can therefore be explained historically by, social facts. If you are not already acquainted with these features, you will learn to know them the more easily if at the same time you learn how they have come into existence.

I will begin with a brief history of the subject. So long as it was supposed that all the peoples of the world denoted relationship in the same way, namely, that which is customary among ourselves, there was no problem. There was no reason why the subject should have awakened any interest, and so far as I have been able to find, it is only since the discovery of the classificatory system of relationship that the problem now before us was ever raised. I imagine that, if students ever thought about the matter at all, it must have seemed obvious that the way in which they and the other known peoples of the world used terms of relationship was conditioned and determined by the social relations which the terms denoted.

The state of affairs became very different as soon as it was known that many peoples of the world use terms of relationship in a manner, and according to rules, so widely different from our own that they seem to belong to an altogether different order, a difference well illustrated by the confusion which is apt to arise when we use English words in the translation of classificatory terms or classificatory terms as the equivalents of our own. The difficulty or impossibility of conforming to complete truth and reality, when we attempt this task, is the best witness to the fundamental difference between the two modes of denoting relationship.

I do not know of any discovery in the whole range of science which can be more certainly put to the credit of one man than that of the classificatory system of relationship by Lewis Morgan. By this I mean, not merely that he was the first to point out clearly the existence of this mode of denoting relationship, but that it was he who collected the vast mass of material by which the essential characters of the system were demonstrated, and it was he who was the first to recognize the great theoretical importance of his new discovery. It is the denial of this importance by his contemporaries and successors which furnishes the best proof of the credit which is due to him for the discovery. The very extent of the material he collected[1] has probably done much to obstruct the recognition of the importance of his work. It is a somewhat discouraging thought that, if Morgan had been less industrious and had amassed a smaller collection of material which could have been embodied in a more available form, the value of his work would probably have been far more widely recognized than it is today. The volume of his material is, however, only a subsidiary factor in the process which has led to the neglect or rejection of the importance of Morgan's discovery. The chief cause of the neglect is one for which Morgan must himself largely bear the blame. He was not content to demonstrate, as he might to some extent have done from his own material, the close connection between the terminology of the classificatory system of relationship and forms of social organization. There can be little doubt that he recognized this connection, but he was not content to demonstrate the dependence of the terminology of relationship upon social forms the existence of which was already known,

[1] *Systems of Consanguinity and Affinity of the Human Family: Smithsonian Contributions to Knowledge*, vol. XVII; Washington, 1871.

or which were capable of demonstration with the material at his disposal. He passed over all these early stages of the argument, and proceeded directly to refer the origin of the terminology to forms of social organization which were not known to exist anywhere on the earth and of which there was no direct evidence in the past. When, further, the social condition which Morgan was led to formulate was one of general promiscuity developing into group-marriage, conditions bitterly repugnant to the sentiments of most civilized persons, it is not surprising that he aroused a mass of heated opposition which led, not merely to widespread rejection of his views, but also to the neglect of lessons to be learnt from his new discovery which must have received general recognition long before this, if they had not been obscured by other issues.

The first to take up the cudgels in opposition to Morgan was our own pioneer in the study of the early forms of human society, John Ferguson McLennan.[1] He criticized the views of Morgan severely and often justly, and then pointing out, as was then believed to be the case, that no duties or rights were connected with the relationships of the classificatory system, he concluded that the terms formed merely a code of courtesies and ceremonial addresses for social intercourse. Those who have followed him have usually been content to repeat the conclusion that the classificatory system is nothing more than a body of mutual salutations and terms of address. They have failed to see that it still remains necessary to explain how the terms of the classificatory system came to be used in mutual salutation. They have failed to recognize that they were either rejecting the principle of determinism in sociology, or were only putting back to a conveniently remote distance the consideration of the problem how and why the classificatory terms came to be used in the way now customary among so many peoples of the earth.

This aspect of the problem, which has been neglected or put on one side by the followers of McLennan, was not so treated by McLennan himself. As we should expect from the general character of his work, McLennan clearly recognized that the classificatory system must have been determined by social conditions, and he tried to show how it might have arisen as the result of the change from the Nair to the Tibetan form of polyandry.[2] He even

[1] *Studies in Ancient History*, 1st series, 1876, p. 331.   [2] *Op. cit.*, p. 373.

went so far as to formulate varieties of this process by means of which there might have been produced the chief varieties of the classificatory system, the existence of which had been demonstrated by Morgan. It is quite clear that McLennan had no doubts about the necessity of tracing back the social institution of the classificatory system of relationship to social causes, a necessity which has been ignored or even explicitly denied by those who have followed him in rejecting the views of Morgan. It is one of the many unfortunate consequences of McLennan's belief in the importance of polyandry in the history of human society that it has helped to prevent his followers from seeing the social importance of the classificatory system. They have failed to see that the classificatory system may be the result neither of promiscuity nor of polyandry, and yet have been determined, both in its general character and in its details, by forms of social organization.

Since the time of Morgan and McLennan few have attempted to deal with the question in any comprehensive manner. The problem has inevitably been involved in the controversy which has raged between the advocates of the original promiscuity or the primitive monogamy of mankind, but most of the former have been ready to accept Morgan's views blindly, while the latter have been content to try to explain away the importance of conclusions derived from the classificatory system without attempting any real study of the evidence. On the side of Morgan there has been one exception in the person of Professor J. Kohler,[1] who has recognized the lines on which the problem must be studied, while on the other side there has been, so far as I am aware, only one writer who has recognized that the evidence from the nature of the classificatory system of relationship cannot be ignored or belittled, but must be faced and some explanation alternative to that of Morgan provided.

This attempt was made four years ago by Professor Kroeber,[2] of the University of California. The line he takes is absolutely to reject the view common to both Morgan and McLennan that the nature of the classificatory system has been determined by social conditions. He explicitly rejects the view that the mode of using terms of relationship depends on social causes, and puts

---

[1] *Zur Urgeschichte der Ehe*, Stuttgart, 1897 (reprinted from *Zeitsch. f. vergleich. Rechtswiss.*, 1897, XII, 187).

[2] *Journ. Roy. Anth. Inst.*, 1909, XXXIX, 77.

D

forward as the alternative that they are conditioned by causes purely linguistic and psychological.

It is not quite easy to understand what is meant by the linguistic causation of terms of relationship. In the summary at the end of his paper Kroeber concludes that 'they (terms of relationship) are determined primarily by language'. Terms of relationship, however, are elements of language, so that Kroeber's proposition is that elements of language are determined primarily by language. In so far as this proposition has any meaning, it must be that, in the process of seeking the origin of linguistic phenomena, it is our business to ignore any but linguistic facts. It would follow that the student of the subject should seek the antecedents of linguistic phenomena in other linguistic phenomena, and put on one side as not germane to his task all reference to the objects and relations which the words denote and connote.

Professor Kroeber's alternative proposition is that terms of relationship reflect psychology, not sociology, or, in other words, that the way in which terms of relationship are used depends on a chain of causation in which psychological processes are the direct antecedents of this use. I will try to make his meaning clear by means of an instance which he himself gives. He says that at the present time there is a tendency among ourselves to speak of the brother-in-law as a brother; in other words, we tend to class the brother-in-law and the brother together in the nomenclature of our own system of relationship. He supposes that we do this because there is a psychological similarity between the two relationships which leads us to class them together in our customary nomenclature. I shall return both to this and other of his examples later.

We have now seen that the opponents of Morgan have taken up two main positions which it is possible to attack: one, that the classificatory system is nothing more than a body of terms of address; the other, that it and other modes of denoting relationship are determined by psychological and not by sociological causes. I propose to consider these two positions in turn.

Morgan himself was evidently deeply impressed by the function of the classificatory system of relationship as a body of salutations. His own experience was derived from the North American Indians, and he notes the exclusive use of terms of relationship in address, a usage so habitual that an omission to recognize a relative in this manner would amount almost to an affront. Morgan also points out, as one motive for the custom, the presence of a reluctance to utter personal names. McLennan had to rely entirely on the evidence collected by Morgan, and there can be no doubt that he was greatly influenced by the stress Morgan himself laid on the function of the classificatory terms as mutual salutations. That in rude societies certain relatives have social functions definitely assigned to them by custom was known in Morgan's time, and I think it might even then have been discovered that the relationships which carried these functions were of the classificatory kind. It is, however, only by more recent work, beginning with that of Howitt, of Spencer and Gillen, and of Roth in Australia, and of the Cambridge Expedition to Torres Straits, that the great importance of the functions of relatives through the classificatory system has been forced upon the attention of sociologists. The social and ceremonial proceedings of the Australian aborigines abound in features in which special functions are performed by such relatives as the elder brother or the brother of the mother, while in Torres Straits I was able to record large groups of duties, privileges and restrictions associated with different classificatory relationships.

Further work has shown that widely, though not universally, the nomenclature of the classificatory system carries with it a number of clearly defined social practices. One who applies a given term of relationship to another person has to behave towards that person in certain definite ways. He has to perform certain duties towards him, and enjoys certain privileges, and is subject to certain restrictions in his conduct in relation to him. These duties, privileges and restrictions vary greatly in number among different peoples, but wherever they exist, I know of no exception to their importance and to the regard in which they are held by all members of the community. You doubtless know of many examples of such functions associated with relationship, and I need give only one example.

In the Banks Islands the term used between two brothers-in-law is *wulus*, *walus*, or *walui*, and a man who applies one of these terms to another may not utter his name, nor may the two behave familiarly towards one another in any way. In one island, Merlav, these relatives have all their possessions in common, and it is the duty of one to help the other in any difficulty, to warn him in danger, and, if need be, to die with him. If one dies, the other has to help to support his widow and has to abstain from certain foods. Further, there are a number of curious regulations in which the sanctity of the head plays a great part. A man must take nothing from above the head of his brother-in-law, nor may he even eat a bird which has flown over his head. A person has only to say of an object 'That is the head of your brother-in-law', and the person addressed will have to desist from the use of the object. If the object is edible, it may not be eaten; if it is one which is being manufactured, such as a mat, the person addressed will have to cease from his work if the object be thus called the head of his brother-in-law. He will only be allowed to finish it on making compensation, not to the person who has prevented the work by reference to the head, but to the brother-in-law whose head had been mentioned. Ludicrous as some of these customs may seem to us, they are very far from being so to those who practise them. They show clearly the very important part taken in the lives of those who use the classificatory system by the social functions associated with relationship. As I have said, these functions are not universally associated with the classificatory system, but they are very general in many parts of the world and only need more careful investigation to be found even more general and more important than appears at present.

Let us now look at our own system of relationship from this point of view. Two striking features present themselves. First, the great paucity of definite social functions associated with relationship, and secondly, the almost complete limitation of such functions to those relationships which apply only to individual persons and not to classes of persons. Of such relationships as cousin, uncle, aunt, father-in-law, or mother-in-law there may be said to be no definite social functions. A schoolboy believes it is the duty of his uncle to tip him, but this is about as near as one can get to any social obligation on the part of this relative.

The same will be found to hold good to a large extent if we turn to those social regulations which have been embodied in our laws. It is only in the case of the transmission of hereditary rank and of the property of a person dying intestate that more distant relatives are brought into any legal relationship with one another, and then only if there is an absence of nearer relatives. It is only when forced to do so by exceptional circumstances that the law recognizes any of the persons to whom the more classificatory of our terms of relationship apply. If we pay regard to the social functions associated with relationship, it is our own system, rather than the classificatory, which is open to the reproach that its relationships carry into them no rights and duties.

In the course of the recent work of the Percy Sladen Trust Expedition in Melanesia and Polynesia I have been able to collect a body of facts which bring out, even more clearly than has hitherto been recognized, the dependence of classificatory terms on social rights.[1] The classificatory systems of Oceania vary greatly in character. In some places relationships are definitely distinguished in nomenclature which are classed with other relationships elsewhere. Thus, while most Melanesian and some Polynesian systems have a definite term for the mother's brother and for the class of relatives whom the mother calls brother, in other systems this relative is classed with, and is denoted by, the same term as the father. The point to which I now call your attention is that there is a very close correlation between the presence of a special term for this relative and the presence of special functions attached to the relationship.

In Polynesia, both the Hawaiians and the inhabitants of Niue class the mother's brother with the father, and in neither place was I able to discover that there were any special duties, privileges or restrictions ascribed to the mother's brother. In the Polynesian islands of Tonga and Tikopia, on the other hand, where there are special terms for the mother's brother, this relative has also special functions. The only place in Melanesia where I failed to find a special term for the mother's brother was in the western Solomon Islands, and that was also the only part of Melanesia where I failed to find any trace of special social functions ascribed to this relative. I do not know of such functions in Santa Cruz, but my information about the system of that island is derived from others, and further research will almost certainly show that they are present.

In my own experience, then, among two different peoples, I have been able to establish a definite correlation between the presence of a term of relationship and special functions associated

[1] The full account of these and other facts cited in these lectures will appear shortly in a work on *The History of Melanesian Society*, to be published by the Cambridge University Press.

with the relationship. Information kindly given to me by Father Egidi, however, seems to show that the correlation among the Melanesians is not complete. In Mekeo, the mother's brother has the duty of putting on the first perineal garment of his nephew, but he has no special term and is classed with the father. Among the Kuni, on the other hand, there is a definite term for the mother's brother distinguishing him from the father, but yet he has not, so far as Father Egidi knows, any special functions.

Both in Melanesia and Polynesia a similar correlation comes out in connection with other relationships, the most prominent exception being the absence of a special term for the father's sister in the Banks Islands, although this relative has very definite and important functions. In these islands the father's sister is classed with the mother as *vev* or *veve*, but even here, where the generalization seems to break down, it does not do so completely, for the father's sister is distinguished from the mother as *veve vus rawe*, the mother who kills a pig, as opposed to the simple *veve* used for the mother and her sisters.

There is thus definite evidence, not only for the association of classificatory terms of relationship with special social functions, but from one part of the world we now have evidence which shows that the presence or absence of special terms is largely dependent on whether there are or are not such functions. We may take it as established that the terms of the classificatory system are not, as McLennan supposed, merely terms of address and modes of mutual salutation. McLennan came to this conclusion because he believed that the classificatory terms were associated with no such functions as those of which we now have abundant evidence. He asks, 'What duties or rights are affected by the relationships comprised in the classificatory system?' and answers himself according to the knowledge at his disposal, 'Absolutely none.'[1] This passage makes it clear that, if McLennan had known what we know today, he would never have taken up the line of attack upon Morgan's position in which he has had, and still has, so many followers.

I can now turn to the second line of attack, that which boldly discards the origin of the terminology of relationship in social conditions, and seeks for its explanation in psychology. The line

[1] *Op. cit.*, p. 366.

of argument I propose to follow is first to show that many details of classificatory systems have been directly determined by social factors. If that task can be accomplished, we shall have firm ground from which to take off in the attempt to refer the general characters of the classificatory and other systems of relationship to forms of social organization. Any complete theory of a social institution has not only to account for its general characters, but also for its details, and I propose to begin with the details.

I must first return to the history of the subject, and stay for a moment to ask why the line of argument I propose to follow was not adopted by Morgan and has been so largely disregarded by others.

Whenever a new phenomenon is discovered in any part of the world, there is a natural tendency to seek for its parallels elsewhere. Morgan lived at a time when the unity of human culture was a topic which greatly excited ethnologists, and it is evident that one of his chief interests in the new discovery arose from the possibility it seemed to open of showing the uniformity of human culture. He hoped to demonstrate the uniformity of the classificatory system throughout the world, and he was content to observe certain broad varieties of the system and refer them to supposed stages in the history of human society. He paid but little attention to such varieties of the classificatory system as are illustrated in his own record of North American systems, and seems to have overlooked entirely certain features of the Indian and Oceanic systems he recorded, which might have enabled him to demonstrate the close relation between the terminology of relationship and social institutions. Morgan's neglect to attend to these differences must be ascribed in some measure to the ignorance of rude forms of social organization which existed when he wrote, but the failure of others to recognize the dependence of the details of classificatory systems upon social institutions is rather to be ascribed to the absence of interest in the subject induced by their adherence to McLennan's primary error. Those who believe that the classificatory system is merely an unimportant code of mutual salutations are not likely to attend to relatively minute differences in the customs they despise. The credit of having been the first fully to recognize the social importance of these differences belongs to J. Kohler. In his book *Zur Urgeschichte der Ehe*, which I have already mentioned, he studied minutely the details of many different systems, and showed that they could be explained by certain forms of marriage practised by those who use the terms. I propose now to deal with classificatory terminology from this point of view. My procedure will be first to show that the details which distinguish different forms of the classificatory system from one another have been directly determined by the social institutions of those who use the systems, and only when this has been established, shall I attempt to bring the more general characters of the classificatory and other systems into relation with social institutions.

I am able to carry out this task more fully than has hitherto been possible because I have collected in Melanesia a number of systems of relationship which differ far more widely from one another than those recorded in Morgan's book or others which have been collected since. Some of the features which characterize these Melanesian systems will be wholly new to ethnologists, not having yet been recorded elsewhere, but I propose to begin with a long familiar mode of terminology which accompanies that widely distributed custom known as the cross-cousin marriage. In the more frequent form of this marriage a man marries the daughter either of his mother's brother or of his father's sister; more rarely his choice is limited to one of these relatives.

Such a marriage will have certain definite consequences. Let us take a case in which a man marries the daugher of his mother's brother, as is represented in the following diagram:

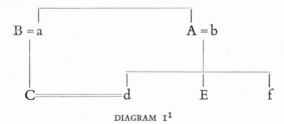

DIAGRAM I[1]

One consequence of the marriage between C and d will be that A, who before the marriage of C was only his mother's brother, now becomes also his wife's father, while b, who before the marriage was the mother's brother's wife of C, now becomes his wife's

[1] In this and other diagrams capital letters are used to represent men and the smaller letters women.

mother. Reciprocally, C, who before his marriage had been the sister's son of A and the husband's sister's son of b, now becomes their son-in-law. Further, E and f, the other children of A and b, who before the marriage had been only the cousins of C, now becomes his wife's brother and sister.

Similarly, a, who before the marriage of d was her father's sister, now becomes also her husband's mother, and B, her father's sister's husband, comes to stand in the relation of husband's father; if C should have any brothers and sisters, these cousins now become her brothers- and sisters-in-law.

The combinations of relationship which follow from the marriage of a man with the daughter of his mother's brother thus differ for a man and a woman, but if, as is usual, a man may marry the daughter either of his mother's brother or of his father's sister, these combinations of relationship will hold good for both men and women.

Another and more remote consequence of the cross-cousin marriage, if this become an established institution, is that the relationships of mother's brother and father's sister's husband will come to be combined in one and the same person, and that there will be a similar combination of the relationships of father's sister and mother's brother's wife. If the cross-cousin marriage be the habitual custom, B and b in Diagram 1 will be brother and sister; in consequence A will be at once the mother's brother and the father's sister's husband of C, while b will be both his father's sister and his mother's brother's wife. Since, however, the mother's brother is also the father-in-law, and the father's sister the mother-in-law, three different relationships will be combined in each case. Through the cross-cousin marriage the relationships of mother's brother, father's sister's husband and father-in-law will be combined in one and the same person, and the relationships of father's sister, mother's brother's wife and mother-in-law will be similarly combined.

In many places where we know the cross-cousin marriage to be an established institution, we find just those common designations which I have just described. Thus, in the Mbau dialect of Fiji the word *vungo* is applied to the mother's brother, the husband of the father's sister and the father-in-law. The word *nganei* is used for the father's sister, the mother's brother's wife and the mother-in-law. The term *tavale* is used by a man for the son of the mother's brother or of the father's sister as well as for the wife's brother and the sister's husband. *Ndavola* is used not only for the child of the mother's brother or father's sister when differing in sex from the speaker, but this word is also used by a man for his wife's sister and his brother's wife, and by a woman for her husband's brother and her sister's husband. Every one of these details of the Mbau system is the direct and inevitable consequence of the cross-cousin marriage, if it becomes an established and habitual practice.

This Fijian system does not stand alone in Melanesia. In the southern islands of the New Hebrides, in Tanna, Eromanga, Aneityum and Aniwa, the cross-cousin marriage is practised and their systems of relationship have features similar to those of Fiji. Thus, in Aneityum the word *matak* applies to the mother's brother, the father's sister's husband and the father-in-law, while the word *engak* used for the cross-cousin is not only used for the wife's sister and the brother's wife, but also for the wife herself.

Again, in the island of Guadalcanal in the Solomons the system of relationship is just such as would result from the cross-cousin marriage. One term, *nia*, is used for the mother's brother and the wife's father, and probably also for the father's sister's husband and the husband's father, though my stay in the island was not long enough to enable me to collect sufficient genealogical material to demonstrate these points completely. Similarly, *tarunga* includes in its connotation the father's sister, the mother's brother's wife and the wife's mother, and probably also the husband's mother, while the word *iva* is used for both cross-cousins and brothers- and sisters-in-law. Corresponding to this terminology there seemed to be no doubt that it was the custom for a man to marry the daughter of his mother's brother or his father's sister though I was not able to demonstrate this form of marriage genealogically.

These three regions, Fiji, the southern New Hebrides and Guadalcanal, are the only parts of Melanesia included in my survey where I found the practice of the cross-cousin marriage, and in all three regions the systems of relationship are just such as would follow from this form of marriage.

Let us now turn to inquire how far it is possible to explain these features of Melanesian systems of relationship by psychological similarity. If it were not for the cross-cousin marriage, what can there be to give the mother's brother a greater psychological similarity to the father-in-law than the father's brother, or the father's sister a greater similarity to the mother-in-law than the mother's sister? Why should it be two special kinds of cousin who are classed with two special kinds of brother- and sister-in-law or with the husband or wife? Once granted the presence of the cross-cousin marriage, and there are psychological similarities certainly, though even here the matter is not quite straight-forward from the point of view of the believer in their import-ance, for we have to do not merely with the similarity of two relatives, but with their identity, with the combination of two or more relationships in one and the same person. Even if we put this on one side, however, it remains to ask how it is possible to say that terms of relationship do not reflect sociology, if such psycho-logical similarities are themselves the result of the cross-cousin marriage? What point is there in bringing in hypothetical psychological similarities which are only at the best intermediate links in the chain of causation connecting the terminology of relationship with antecedent social conditions?

If you concede the causal relation between the characteristic features of a Fijian or Aneityum or Guadalcanal system and the cross-cousin marriage, there can be no question that it is the cross-cousin marriage which is the antecedent and the features of the system of relationship the consequences. I do not suppose that, even in this subject, there will be found anyone to claim that the Fijians took to marrying their cross-cousins because such a marriage was suggested to them by the nature of their system of relationship. We have to do in this case, not merely with one or two features which might be the consequence of the cross-cousin marriage, but with a large and complicated meshwork of re-semblances and differences in the nomenclature of relationship, each and every element of which follows directly from such a marriage, while no one of the systems I have considered possesses a single feature which is not compatible with social conditions arising out of this marriage. Apart from quantitative verification, I doubt whether it would be possible in the whole range of science to find a case where we can be more confident that one pheno-menon has been conditioned by another. I feel almost guilty of wasting your time by going into it so fully, and should hardly have ventured to do so if this case of social causation had not been explicitly denied by one with so high a reputation as Professor

Kroeber. I hope, however, that the argument will be useful as an example of the method I shall apply to other cases in which the evidence is less conclusive.

The features of terminology which follow from the cross-cousin marriage were known to Morgan, being present in three of the systems he recorded from Southern India and in the Fijian system collected for him by Mr Fison. The earliest reference[1] to the cross-cousin marriage which I have been able to discover is among the Gond of Central India. This marriage was recorded in 1870, which, though earlier than the appearance of Morgan's book, was after it had been accepted for publication, so that I think we can be confident that Morgan was unacquainted with the form of marriage which would have explained the peculiar features of the Indian and Fijian systems. It is evident, however, that Morgan was so absorbed in his demonstration of the similarity of these systems to those of America that he paid but little, if any, attention to their peculiarities. He thus lost a great opportunity; if he had attended to these peculiarities and had seen their meaning, he might have predicted a form of marriage which would soon afterwards have been independently discovered. Such an example of successful prediction would have forced the social significance of the terminology of relationship upon the attention of students in such a way that we should have been spared much of the controversy which has so long obstructed progress in this branch of sociology. It must at the very least have acted as a stimulus to the collection of systems of relationship. It would hardly have been possible that now, more than forty years after the appearance of Morgan's book, we are still in complete ignorance of the terminology of relationship of many peoples about whom volumes have been written. It would seem impossible, for instance, that our knowledge of Indian systems of relationship could have been what it is today. India would have been the country in which the success of Morgan's prediction would first have shown itself, and such an event must have prevented the almost total neglect which the subject of relationship has suffered at the hands of students of Indian sociology.

[1] Grant, *Gazetteer of Central Provinces*, Nagpur, 2nd ed., 1870, p. 276.

Lecture 2

In my last lecture I began the demonstration of the dependence of the classificatory terminology of relationship upon social institutions by showing how a number of terms used in several parts of Melanesia have been determined by the cross-cousin marriage. I showed that in places where the cross-cousin marriage is practised there are not merely one or two, but large groups of, terms of relationship which are exactly such as would follow from this form of marriage. Today I begin by considering other forms of Melanesian marriage which bring out almost as clearly and conclusively the dependence of the classificatory terminology upon social conditions.

The systems of relationship of the Banks Islands possess certain very remarkable features which were first recorded by Dr Codrington.[1] Put very shortly, it may be stated that cross-cousins stand to one another in the relation of parent and child, or, more exactly, cross-cousins apply to one another terms of relationship which are otherwise used between parents and children. A man applies to his mother's brother's children the term which he otherwise uses for his own children, and, conversely, a person applies to his father's sister's son a term he otherwise uses for his father. Thus, in the following diagram, C will apply to D and e the terms which are in general use for a son and daughter, while D and e will apply to C the term they otherwise use for their father.

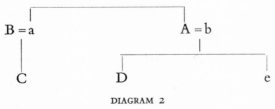

DIAGRAM 2

---

[1] *The Melanesians*, p. 38.

In most forms of the classificatory system members of different generations are denoted in wholly different ways and belong to different classes,[1] but here we have a case in which persons of the same generation as the speaker are classed with those of an older generation or a younger generation.

I will first ask you to consider to what kind of psychological similarity such a practice can be due. What kind of psychological similarity can there be between one special kind of cousin and the father, and between another special kind of cousin and a son or daughter? If the puzzle as put in this form does not seem capable of a satisfactory answer, let us turn to see if the Banks Islanders practise any social custom to which this peculiar terminology can have been due. In the story of Ganviviris told to Dr Codrington in these islands[2] an incident occurs in which a man hands over one of his wives to his sister's son, or, in other words, in which a man marries one of the wives of his mother's brother. Inquiries showed, not only that this form of marriage was once widely current in the islands, but that it still persists though in a modified form. The Christianity of the natives does not now permit a man to have superfluous wives whom he can pass on to his sister's sons, but it is still the orthodox, and indeed I was told the popular, custom to marry the widow of the mother's brother. It seemed that in the old days a man would take the widow of his mother's brother in addition to any wife or wives he might already have. Though this is no longer allowed, the leaning towards this form of marriage is so strong that after fifty years of external influence a young man still marries the widow of his mother's brother, sometimes in preference to a girl of his own age. Indeed, there was reason to believe that there was an obligation to do so, if the deceased husband had a nephew who was not yet married. The peculiar features of the terminology of relationship in these islands are exactly such as would follow from this form of marriage. If, in Diagram 2, C marries b, the wife or widow of his mother's brother, and thereby comes to occupy the social position of his uncle A, the children of the uncle, D and e, will come to stand to him in the relation of children, while he, who had previously been the father's sister's son of D and e, will now become their father.

---

[1] I leave out of account here those cases in which members of different generations are denoted by a reciprocal term.

[2] *Op. cit.*, p. 384.

An exceptional form of the classificatory system, in which there is a departure from the usual rule limiting a term of relationship to members of the same generation, is found to be the natural consequence of a social regulation which enjoins the marriage of persons belonging to different generations.

The next step in the process of demonstrating the social significance of the classificatory system of relationship will take us to the island of Pentecost in the northern New Hebrides. When I recorded the system of this island, I found it to have so bizarre and complex a character that I could hardly believe at first it could be other than the result of a ludicrous misunderstanding between myself and my seemingly intelligent and trustworthy informants. Nevertheless, the records obtained from two independent witnesses, and based on separate pedigrees, agreed so closely even in the details which seemed most improbable that I felt confident that the whole construction could not be so mad as it seemed. This confidence was strengthened by finding that some of its features were of the same order of peculiarity as others which I had already found in a set of Fijian systems I have yet to consider. There were certain features which brought relatives separated by two generations into one category; the mother's mother, for instance, received the same designation as the elder sister; the wife's mother the same as the daughter; the wife's brother the same as the daughter's son. The only conclusion I was then able to formulate was that these features were the result of some social institution resembling the matrimonial classes of Australia, which would have the effect of putting persons of alternate generations into one social category.

This idea was supported by the system of relationship of the Dieri of Australia which possesses at least one feature similar to those of Pentecost, a fact I happened to remember at the time because Mr N. W. Thomas[1] had used it as the basis of a *reductio ad absurdum* argument to show that terms of relationship do not express kinship. The interest of the Pentecost system seemed at first to lie in the possibility thus opened of bringing Melanesian into relation with Australian sociology, a hope which was the more promising in that the people of Pentecost and the Dieri resemble one another in the general character of their social

[1] *Kinship Organisations and Group Marriage in Australia*, Cambridge, 1906, p. 123.

organization, each being organized on the dual basis with matrilineal descent. When in Pentecost, however, I was unable to get further than this, and the details of the system remained wholly inexplicable.

The meaning of some of the peculiarities of the Pentecost system became clear when I reached the Banks Islands; they were of the same kind as those I have already considered as characteristic of these islands. When I had discovered the dependence of these features upon the marriage of a man with the wife of his mother's brother, it became evident that not only these, but certain other features of the Pentecost system, were capable of being accounted for by this kind of marriage. The peculiar features of the Pentecost system could be divided into two groups, and all the members of one group could be accounted for by the marriage with the mother's brother's wife. All these features had the character in common that persons of the generation immediately above or below that of the speaker were classed in nomenclature with relatives of the same generation.

The other group consisted of terms in which persons two generations apart were classed with relatives of the same generation. Since the first group of correspondences had been explained by a marriage between persons one generation apart, it should have been obvious that the classing together of persons two generations apart might have been the result of marriage between persons two generations apart. The idea of a society in which marriages between those having the status of grandparents and grandchildren were habitual must have seemed so unlikely that, if it entered my mind at all, it must have been at once dismissed. The clue only came later from a man named John Pantutun, a native of the Banks Islands, who had been a teacher in Pentecost. In talking to me he often mentioned in a most instructive manner resemblances and differences between the customs of his own island and those he had observed in Pentecost. One day he let fall the observation with just such a manner as that in which we so often accuse neighbouring nations of ridiculous or disgusting practices, 'O! Raga![1] That is the place where they marry their granddaughters.' I saw at once that he had given me a possible explanation of the peculiar features of the system of the island. By that time I had forgotten the details of the Pentecost system,

[1] This is the Mota name for Pentecost Island.

and it occurred to me that it would be interesting, not immediately to consult my note-books, but to endeavour to construct a system of relationship which would be the result of marriage with a granddaughter, and then to see how far my theoretical construction agreed with the terminology I had recorded. The first question which arose was with which kind of granddaughter the marriage had been practised, with the son's daughter or with the daughter's daughter, and this was a question readily answered by means of a consideration arising out of the nature of the social organization of Pentecost.

The society of this island is organized on the dual basis with matrilineal descent in which a man must marry a woman of the opposite moiety. Diagram 3, in which A and a stand for men and

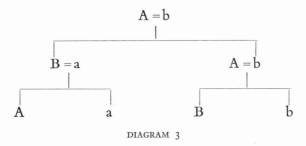

DIAGRAM 3

women of one moiety, and B and b for those of the other moiety, shows that a marriage between a man and his son's daughter would be out of the question, for it would be a case of A marrying a. It was evident that the marriage, the consequences of which I had to formulate, must have been one in which a man married his daughter's daughter.

It would take too long to go through the whole set of relationships, and I choose only a few examples which I illustrate by the following diagram:

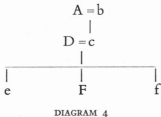

DIAGRAM 4

E

This diagram shows that if A marries e, c, who previous to the marriage had been only the daughter of A, now becomes also his wife's mother; and D, who had previously been his daughter's husband, now becomes his wife's father. Similarly, F, who before the new marriage was the daughter's son of A, now becomes the brother of his wife, while f, his daughter's daughter, becomes his wife's sister. Lastly, if we assume that it would be the elder daughters of the daughter who would be married by their grandfathers, e, who before the marriage had been the elder sister of F and f, now comes through her marriage to occupy the position of their mother's mother.

When, after making these deductions, I examined my record of the Pentecost terms, I found that its terminology corresponded exactly with those which had been deduced. The wife's mother and the daughter were both called *nitu*. The daughter's husband and the wife's father were both *bwaliga*. The daughter's children were called *mabi*, and this term was also used for the brother and sister of the wife. Lastly, the mother's mother was found to be classed with the elder sister, both being called *tuaga*.

For the sake of simplicity of demonstration I have assumed that a man marries his own daughter's daughter, but through the classificatory principle all the features I have described would follow equally well if a man married the granddaughter of his brother, either in the narrow or the classificatory sense. There was one correspondence, according to which both the husband's brother and the mother's father were called *sibi*, which does not follow from the marriage with the own granddaughter, but would be the natural result of marriage with the daughter's daughter of the brother—i.e., with a marriage in which e was married by A's brother.

I hope these examples will be sufficient to show how a number of features which might otherwise seem so absurd as to suggest a system of relationship gone mad become natural and intelligible, even obvious, if it were once the established practice of the people to marry the daughter's daughter of the brother.

Such inquiries as I was able to make confirmed the conclusion that the Pentecost marriage was with the granddaughter of the brother rather than with the daughter of the daughter herself. After I had been put on the track of the explanation by John Pantutun I had the chance of talking to only one native of Pentecost, unfortunately not a very good informant. From his evidence it appeared that the marriage I had inferred from the system of relationship even now occurs in the island, but only with the granddaughter of the brother, and that marriage with the own granddaughter is forbidden. The evidence is not as complete as I should like, but it points to the actual existence in the island of a peculiar form of marriage from which the extraordinary features of its system of relationship directly follow.

When I returned to England I found that this marriage was not unique, but had been recorded among the Dieri of Australia,[1] where, as I have already mentioned, it is associated with peculiar features of nomenclature resembling those of Pentecost.

I must again ask, how are you going to explain the features of the Pentecost system psychologically? What psychological resemblance is there between a grandmother and a sister, between a mother-in-law and a daughter, between a brother-in-law and a grandfather? Apart from some special form of social relationship, there can be no such resemblances. Further, if there were such psychological resemblances, why should we know of their influence on nomenclature only in Pentecost and among the Dieri? The features to be explained are definitely known to exist in only two systems of the world, and it is only among the peoples who use these two systems that we have any evidence of that extraordinary form of marriage of which they would be the natural consequence.

I have now tried to show the dependence of special features of the classificatory system of relationship upon special social conditions. If I have succeeded in this I shall have gone far towards the accomplishment of one of the main purposes of these lectures. They have, however, another purpose, viz., to inquire how far we are justified in inferring the existence of a social institution of which we have no direct evidence when we find features of the nomenclature of relationship which would result from such an institution. I have now to enter upon this part of my subject, and I think it will be instructive to take you at once to a case in which I believe that an extraordinary form of marriage can be established as a feature of the past history of a people, although at the

[1] Howitt, *Native Tribes of South-East Australia*, pp. 164, 177.

present moment any direct evidence for the existence of such a marriage is wholly lacking.

When I was in the interior of Viti Levu, one of the Fijian islands, I discovered the existence of certain systems of relationship which differed fundamentally from the only Fijian systems previously known. Any features referable to the cross-cousin marriage were completely absent, but in their place were others, one of which I have already mentioned, which brought into one class relatives two generations apart. The father's father received the same designation as the elder brother, and the son's wife was called by the same term as the mother. As I have already said, my first conclusion was that these terms were the survivals of forms of social organization resembling the matrimonial classes of Australia, but as soon as I had worked out the explanation of the Pentecost system, it became evident that the Fijian peculiarities would have to be explained on similar lines. At first I thought it probable that the difference between the Pentecost and Fijian systems was due to the difference in the mode of descent in the two places. For long I tried to work out schemes whereby a change from the matrilineal descent of Pentecost to the patrilineal condition of Fiji could have had as one of its consequences a change from a correspondence in nomenclature between the mother's mother and the elder sister to one in which the common nomenclature applied to the father's father and the elder brother. It is an interesting example of the strength of a preconceived opinion, and of some measure of the belief in the impossibility of customs not practised by ourselves, that for more than two years I failed to see an obvious alternative explanation, although I returned to the subject again and again. The clue came at last from the system of Buin, in the island of Bougainville, recorded by Dr Thurnwald.[1] The nomenclature of this system agreed with that of inland Fiji in having one term for the father's father and the elder brother, but since the people of Buin still practise matrilineal descent, it was evident that I had been on a false track in supposing the correspondence to have been the result of a change in the mode of descent. Once turned into a fresh path by the necessity of showing how the correspondence could have arisen out of a matrilineal condition, it was not long before I saw how it might be accounted for in a very different way. I saw

[1] *Zeitsch. f. vergleich. Rechtswiss.*, 1910, XXIII, 330.

that the correspondence would be the natural result of a form of social organization in which it was the practice to marry a grandmother, viz., the wife of the father's father. Not only did this form of marriage explain the second peculiar feature of the Fijian system, viz., the classing of the son's wife with the mother, but it would also account for several features of the Buin system which would otherwise be difficult to understand.

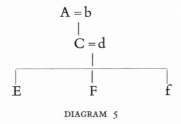

DIAGRAM 5

If, as shown in Diagram 5, E marries b, the wife or widow of his father's father, he who had previously been the elder brother of F and f, now comes to occupy the position of their father's father, while d, the mother of E, will now come to stand to him in the relationship of son's wife.

I need only mention here one of the features of the Buin system which can be accounted for by means of this marriage. The term *mamai* is used, not only for the elder sister and for the elder brother's wife, but it is also applied to the father's mother; that is, the wife of the elder brother is designated by the same term as the wife of the father's father, exactly as must happen if E marries b, the wife of his father's father. A number of extraordinary features from two Melanesian islands collected by two independent workers fit into a coherent scheme if they have been the result of a marriage in which a man gives one of his wives to his son's son during his life, or in which this woman is taken to wife by her husband's grandson when she becomes a widow. If the practice were ever sufficiently habitual to become the basis of the system of relationship, we can be confident that it is the former of these two alternatives with which we have to do.

If you are still so under the domination of ideas derived from your own social surroundings that you cannot believe in such a marriage, I would remind you that there is definite evidence from the Banks Islands that men used to hand over wives to their sisters' sons. It is not taking us so much into the unknown as it might appear to suppose that they once also gave their wives to their sons' sons.

I have taken this case somewhat out of its proper place in my argument because the evidence is so closely connected with that by means of which I have shown the relation between features of systems of relationship and peculiar forms of marriage in Melanesia. I have now to return to the more sober task of considering how far we are justified in inferring the former existence of marriage institutions when we find features of systems of relationship of which they would have been the natural consequence. It is evident that, whenever we find such a feature as common nomenclature for a grandmother and a sister or for a cross-cousin and a parent, it should suggest to us the possibility of such marriage regulations as those of Pentecost and the Banks Islands. But such common designations might have arisen in some other way, and in order to establish the existence of such forms of marriage in the past history of the people, we must have criteria to guide us when we are considering whether a given feature of the terminology of relationship is or is not a survival of a marriage institution.

I will return to the cross-cousin marriage for my examples. The task before us is to inquire how far such features of relationship as exist in Fiji, Aneityum or Guadalcanal, in conjunction with the cross-cousin marriage, will justify us in inferring the former existence of this form of marriage in places where it is not now practised.

If there be found among any people all the characteristic features of a coastal Fijian or of an Aneityum system, I think few will be found to doubt the former existence of the cross-cousin marriage. It would seem almost inconceivable that there should ever have existed any other conditions, whether social or psychological, which could have produced this special combination of peculiar uses of terms of relationship. It is when some only of these features are present that there will arise any serious doubt whether they are to be regarded as survivals of the former existence of the cross-cousin marriage.

One consideration I must point out at once. Certain of the features which follow from the cross-cousin marriage may be the result of another marriage regulation. In some parts of the world there exists a custom of exchanging brothers and sisters, so that, when a man marries a woman, his sister marries his wife's brother. As the result of this custom the mother's brother and the father's sister's husband will come to be one and the same person, and the father's sister will become also the mother's brother's wife.

This form of marriage exists among the western people of Torres Straits,[1] and is accompanied by features of the system of relationship which would follow from the practice. The mother's brother is classed with the father's sister's husband as *wadwam*, but there is an alternative term for the father's sister's husband and there was no evidence that the mother's brother's wife was classed with the father's sister. It seemed possible that the classing together of the mother's brother and the father's sister's husband was not a constant feature of the system of relationship, but only occurred in cases where the custom of exchange had made it necessary. The case, however, is sufficient to show that two of the correspondences which follow from the cross-cousin marriage may be the result of another kind of marriage. If we accept the social causation of such features and find these correspondences alone, it would still remain an open question whether they were the results of the custom of exchange or of the marriage of cross-cousins. The custom of exchange, however, is wholly incapable of accounting for the use of a common term for the mother's brother and the father-in-law, for the father's sister and the mother-in-law, or for cross-cousins and brothers- or sisters-in-law. It is only when these correspondences are present that there will be any decisive reason for inferring the former existence of the cross-cousin marriage.

The first conclusion, then, is that some of the features found in association with the cross-cousin marriage are of greater value than others in enabling us to infer the former existence of the cross-cousin marriage where it no longer exists. Next, the probability that such features as I am considering are due to the former presence of the cross-cousin marriage will be greatly heightened if this form of marriage should exist among people with allied cultures. An instance from Melanesia will bring out this point clearly.

In the island of Florida in the Solomons it is clear that the cross-cousin marriage is not now the custom, and I could discover no tradition of its existence in the past. One feature, however, of the

---

[1] *Rep. Cambridge Expedition to Torres Straits*, vol. v, pp. 135 and 241.

system of relationship is just such as would follow from the cross-cousin marriage. Both the wife's mother and the wife of the mother's brother are called *vungo*.

Florida is not only near Guadalcanal where the cross-cousin marriage is practised (the two islands are within sight of one another), but their cultures are very closely related. In such a case the probability that the single feature of the Florida system which follows from the cross-cousin marriage has actually had that form of marriage as its antecendent becomes very great, and this conclusion becomes still more probable when we find that in a third island, Ysabel, closely allied in culture both to Florida and Guadalcanal, there is a clear tradition of the former practice of the cross-cousin marriage although it is now only an occasional event.

Again, in one district of San Cristobal in the Solomons the term *fongo* is used both for the father-in-law and the father's sister's husband, and *kafongo* similarly denotes both the mother-in-law and the mother's brother's wife. This island differs more widely from Guadalcanal in culture than Florida or Ysabel, but the evidence for the former existence of the marriage in these islands gives us more confidence in ascribing the common designations of San Cristobal to the cross-cousin marriage than would have been the case if these common designations had been the only examples of such possible survivals in the Solomons. Speaking in more general terms, one may say that the probability that the common nomenclature for two relatives is the survival of a form of marriage becomes the greater, the more similar is the general culture in which the supposed survival is found to that of a people who practise this form of marriage. The case will be greatly strengthened if there should be intermediate links between the supposed survival and the still living institution.

When we find a feature such as that of the Florida system among a people none of whose allies in culture practise the cross-cousin marriage, the matter must be far more doubtful. In the present state of our knowledge we are only justified in making such a feature the basis of a working hypothesis to stimulate research and encourage us to look for other evidence in the neighbourhood of the place where the feature has been found. Our knowledge of the social institutions of the world is not yet so complete that we can afford to neglect any clue which may guide our steps.

I propose briefly to consider two regions, South India and North America, to show how they differ from this point of view.

The terms of relationship used in three[1] of the chief languages spoken by the people of South India are exactly such as would follow from the cross-cousin marriage. In Tamil[2] the mother's brother, the father's sister's husband, and the father of both husband and wife are all called *mama*, and this term is also used for these relatives in Telegu. In Canarese the mother's brother and the father-in-law are both called *nava*, but the father's sister's husband fails to fall into line and is classed with the father's brother.

Similarly, the father's sister, the mother's brother's wife and the mother of both wife and husband are called *atta* in Telegu and *atte* in Canarese, Tamil here spoiling the harmony by having one term, *attai*, for the father's sister and another, *mami*, for the mother's brother's wife and the mother-in-law. Since, however, the Tamil term for the father's sister is only another form of the Telegu and Canarese words for the combined relationships, the exception only serves to strengthen the agreement with the condition which would follow from the cross-cousin marriage.

The South Indian terms for cross-cousin and brother- and sister-in-law are complicated by the presence of distinctions dependent on the sex and relative age of those who use them, but these complications do not disguise how definitely the terminology would follow from the cross-cousin marriage. Thus, to take only two examples: a Tamil man applies the term *maittuni* to the daughters of his mother's brother and of his father's sister as well as to his brother's wife and his wife's sister, and a Canarese woman uses one term for the sons of her mother's brother and of her father's sister, for her husband's brother and her sister's husband.

So far as we know, the cross-cousin marriage is not now practised by the vast majority of those who use these terms of relationship. If the terminology has been the result of the cross-cousin marriage, it is only a survival of an ancient social condition in

[1] I know of no complete record of the terminology of the fourth chief language of South India, Malayalam.

[2] I take my data from the lists compiled for Morgan by the Rev. E. C. Scudder and the Rev. B. Rice, Morgan's *Systems...*, pp. 537–66. These lists are not complete, giving in some cases only the terms used in address. They agree in general with some lists compiled during the recent Indian Census which Mr E. A. Gait has kindly sent to me.

which this form of marriage was habitual. That it is such a sur-vival, however, becomes certain when we find the cross-cousin marriage still persisting in many parts of South India, and that among one such people at least, the Todas,[1] this form of marriage is associated with a system of relationship agreeing both in its structure and linguistic character with that of the Tamils. I have elsewhere[2] brought together the evidence for the former preva-lence of this form of marriage in India, but even if there were no evidence, the terminology of relationship is so exactly such as would follow from the cross-cousin marriage that we can be certain that this form of marriage was once the habitual custom of the people of South India.

While South India thus provides a good example of a case in which we can confidently infer the former existence of the cross-cousin marriage from the terminology of relationship, the evidence from North America is of a kind which gives to such an inference only a certain degree of probability. In this case it is necessary to suspend judgment and await further evidence before coming to a positive conclusion.

I will begin with a very doubtful feature which comes from an Athabascan tribe, the Red Knives[3] (probably that now called Yellow Knife). These people use a common term, *set-so*, for the father's sister, the mother's brother's wife, the wife's mother and the husband's mother, a usage which would be the necessary result of the cross-cousin marriage. Against this, however, is to be put the fact that there are three different terms for the corre-sponding male relatives, the two kinds of father-in-law being called *seth-a*, the mother's brother *ser-a*, and the father's sister's husband *selthe-ne*. Further, the term *set-so*, the common use of which for the aunt and mother-in-law seems to indicate the cross-cousin marriage, is also applied by a man to his brother's wife and his wife's sister, features which cannot possibly be the result of this form of marriage. These features show, either that the terminology has arisen in some other way, or that there has been some additional social factor in operation which has greatly modified a nomenclature derived from the cross-cousin marriage.

A stronger case is presented by the terminology of three

---

[1] Rivers, *The Todas*, 1906, pp. 487, 512.
[2] *Journal Royal Asiatic Society*, 1907, p. 611.
[3] See Morgan, *Systems...*, Table II.

branches of the Cree tribe, also recorded by Morgan. In all three systems, one term, *ne-sis* or *nee-sis*, is used for the mother's brother, the father's sister's husband, the wife's father and the husband's father; while the term *nis-si-goos* applies to the father's sister, the mother's brother's wife and the two kinds of mother-in-law. These usages are exactly such as would follow from the cross-cousin marriage. The terms for the sister's son of a man and the brother's son of a woman, however, differ from those used for the son-in-law, and there is also no correspondence between the terms for cross-cousin and any kind of brother- or sister-in-law. The case points more definitely to the cross-cousin marriage than in the case of the Red Knives, but yet lacks the completeness which would allow us to make the inference with confidence.

The Assiniboin have a common term, *me-toh-we*, used for the father's sister, the mother's brother's wife and the two kinds of mother-in-law, and also a common term, *me-nake-she*, for the mother's brother and the father's sister's husband, but the latter differs from the word, *me-to-ga-she*, used for the father of husband or wife. The case here is decidedly stronger than among the Red Knives, but is less complete than among the Cree.

Among a number of branches of the Dakota the evidence is of a different kind, being derived from similar nomenclature for the cross-cousin and certain kinds of brother- and sister-in-law. Morgan[1] has recorded eight systems, all of which show the features in question, but I will consider here only that of the Isauntie or Santee Dakota, which was collected for him by the Rev. S. R. Riggs. Riggs[2] and Dorsey[3] have given independent accounts of this system which are far less complete than that given by Morgan, but agree with it in all essentials.

In this system a man calls the son of his mother's brother or of his father's sister *ta-hang-she* or *tang-hang-she*, while his wife's brother and his sister's husband are *ta-hang* or *tang-hang*. Similarly, a woman calls her cross-cousin *she-chay-she*, while her husband's brother and her sister's husband are called *she-chay*. The terms for brothers-in-law are thus the same as those for cross-cousins with the omission of the suffix *she*. One of these resemblances, that

---

[1] *Loc. cit.*

[2] *Dakota Grammar, Texts, and Ethnography: Contributions to North American Ethnology*, Washington, vol. IX.

[3] Preface to above.

when a woman is speaking, has been cited by Professor Kroeber[1] as an example of the psychological causation of such features of relationship as I am considering in these lectures. He rejects its dependence on the cross-cousin marriage and refers the resemblance to the psychological similarity between a woman's cousin and her brother-in-law in that both are collateral relatives alike in sex, of the same generation as the speaker, but different from her in sex.

As we have seen, however, the Dakota correspondence is not an isolated occurrence, but fits in with a number of other features of the systems of cognate peoples to form a body of evidence pointing to the former prevalence of the cross-cousin marriage.

There is also indirect evidence leading in the same direction. In Melanesia there is reason to believe that the cross-cousin marriage stands in a definite relation to another form of marriage, that with the wife of the mother's brother. If there should be evidence for the former existence of this marriage in North America, it would increase the probability in favour of the cross-cousin marriage.

Among a number of peoples, some of whom form part of the Sioux, including the Minnitaree, Crow, Choctaw, Creek, Cherokee and Pawnee, cross-cousins are classed with parents and children exactly as in the Banks Islands, and exactly as in those islands, it is the son of the father's sister who is classed with the father, and the children of the mother's brother who are classed with sons or daughters. Further, among the Pawnee the wife of the mother's brother is classed with the wife, a feature also associated with the peculiar nomenclature for cross-cousins in the Banks Islands. The agreement is so close as to make it highly probable that the American features of relationship have been derived from a social institution of the same kind as that to which the Melanesian features are due, and that it was once the custom of these American peoples to marry the wife of the mother's brother. Here, as in the case of the cross-cousin marriage itself, the case rests entirely upon the terminology of relationship, but we cannot ignore the association in neighbouring parts of North America of features of relationship which would be the natural consequence of two forms of marriage which are known to be associated together elsewhere.

[1] *Op. cit.*, p. 82.

I am indebted to Miss Freire-Marreco for the information that the Tewa of Hano, a Pueblo tribe, call the father's sister's son *tada*, a term otherwise used for the father, thus suggesting that they also may once have practised marriage with the wife of the mother's brother. The use of this term, however, is only one example of a practice whereby all the males of the father's clan are called *tada*, irrespective of age and generation. The common nomenclature for the father and the father's sister's son among the Tewa thus differs in character from the apparently similar nomenclature of the Banks Islands and cannot have been determined directly, perhaps not even remotely, by marriage with the wife of the mother's brother. This raises the question whether the nomenclature of the Sioux has not arisen out of a practice similar to that of the Tewa. The terms for other relatives recorded by Morgan show some evidence of the widely generalized use of the Tewa, but such a use cannot account for the classing of the wife of the mother's brother with the wife which occurs among the Pawnee. Nevertheless, the Tewa practice should keep us alive to the possibility that the Sioux nomenclature may depend on some social condition different from that which has been effective in the Banks Islands in spite of the close resemblance between the two.

The case for the former existence of the cross-cousin marriage will be much strengthened if this form of marriage should occur elsewhere in North America. So far as I am aware, the only people among whom it has been recorded are the Haida of Queen Charlotte Island.[1] It is a far cry from this outpost of North American culture to Dakota, but it may be noted that it is among the Cree who formerly lived in the intermediate region of Manitoba and Assiniboin that the traces of the cross-cousin marriage are most definite. This mode of distribution of the peoples whose terminology of relationship bears evidence of the cross-cousin marriage suggests that other intermediate links may yet be found. Though the existing evidence is inconclusive, it should be sufficient to stimulate a search for other evidence which may make it possible to decide whether or no the cross-cousin marriage was once a widespread practice in North America.

I can only consider one other kind of marriage here. The

[1] Swanton, *Contributions to the Ethnology of the Haidahs, Jesup North Pacific Expedition*, 1905, vol. v, pt. I, p. 62. Miss Freire-Marreco tells me that the cross-cousin marriage occurs among some of the Hopi Indians.

discovery of so remarkable a union as that with the daughter's daughter in Pentecost and the evidence pointing to a still more remarkable marriage between those having the status of grand-parent and grandchild in Fiji and Buin have naturally led me to look for similar evidence elsewhere in Melanesia. Though there is nothing conclusive, conditions are to be found here and there which suggest the former existence of such marriages.

When I was in the Solomons I met a native of the Trobriand Islands, who told me that among his people the term *tabu* was applied both to grandparents and to the father's sister's child. I went into the whole subject as fully as was possible with only one witness, but in spite of his obvious intelligence and good faith, I remained doubtful whether the information was correct. The feature in question, however, occurs in the list of Trobriand terms drawn up for Dr Seligmann[1] by Mr Bellamy, and with this double warrant it must be accepted. It is a feature which would follow from marriage with the daughter's daughter, for by this marriage one who was previously a father's sister's daughter becomes the wife of a grandfather and thereby attains the status of a grandparent. The feature exists alone, and, further, it is com-bined with other applications of the term which deprive it of some of its significance; nevertheless, the fact that a peculiar and exceptional feature of a Melanesian system of relationship is such as would follow naturally from a form of marriage which is practised in another part of Melanesia cannot be passed over. Standing alone, it would be wholly insufficient to justify the con-clusion that the marriage with the daughter's daughter was ever prevalent among the Massim, but in place of expressing a dog-matic denial, let us look for other features of Massim sociology which may have been the results of such a marriage.

In Wagawaga[2] there is a peculiar term, *warihi*, which is used by men for other men of their own generation and social group, but the term is also applied by an old man or woman to one of a younger generation. Again, in Tubetube[3] the term for a husband, *taubara*, is also a term for an old man, and the term for the wife is also applied to an old woman. These usages may be nothing more than indications of respect for a husband or wife, or of some mechanism which brought those differing widely in age into

---

[1] See *The Melanesians of British New Guinea*, Cambridge, 1910, p. 707.
[2] *Ibid.*, pp. 482 and 436.   [3] *Ibid.*, p. 482.

one social category, but with the clue provided by the Trobriand term of relationship it becomes possible, though even now only possible, that the Wagawaga and Tubetube customs may have arisen out of a social condition in which it was customary to have great disparity of age between husbands and wives, and social relations between old and young following from such disparity in the age of consorts.

In Tubetube there is yet another piece of evidence. Mr Field[1] has recorded the existence in this island of three named categories of persons, two of which comprise relatives with whom marriage is prohibited, while the third groups together those with whom marriage is allowed. The grandparents and grandchildren are included in one of the two prohibited classes, so that we can be confident that marriage between these relatives does not now occur. The point to which I call your attention is that the class of relative with whom marriage is allowed is called *kasoriegogoli*. *Li* is the third person pronominal suffix, and we do not know the meaning of *kasorie*, but *goga* is the term used in Wagawaga and Wedau for the grandparents, its place being taken by the usual Melanesian term *tubu* in Tubetube. The term *kasoriegogoli* applied to marriageable relatives thus contains as one of its constituent elements a word which is probably the ancient term for grandparent in the island, since it is still used in this sense in the closely allied societies of the mainland.

We have thus a number of independent facts among the Massim, all of which would be the natural outcome of marriage between persons of alternate generations. To no one of them standing alone could much importance be attached, but taken in conjunction, they ought at least to suggest the possibility of such a marriage, a possibility which becomes the more probable when we consider that the Massim show clear evidence of the dual organization of society with matrilineal descent which is associated with the granddaughter marriage of Pentecost and the Dieri of Australia. It adds to the weight of the evidence that indications of this peculiar form of marriage should be found among a people whose social organization so closely resembles that in which the marriages between persons of alternate generations elsewhere occur.

I have no time for other examples. I hope to have shown that

[1] Rep. Austral. Ass., 1900, VIII, 301.

there are cases in which it is possible to infer with certainty the ancient existence of forms of marriage from the survival of their results in the terminology of relationship. In other cases, differences of culture or the absence of intermediate links make it unjustifiable to infer the ancient existence of the forms of marriage from which features of terminology might be derived. Other cases lie between the two, the confidence with which a form of marriage can be inferred varying with the degree of likeness of culture, the distance in space, and the presence or absence of other features of culture which may be related to the form of marriage in question. Even in the cases, however, where the inference is most doubtful, we have no right dogmatically to deny the origin of the terminology of relationship in social conditions, but should keep each example before an open mind, to guide and stimulate inquiry in a region where ethnologists have till now only scratched the surface covering a rich mine of knowledge.

Lecture 3

Thus far in these lectures I have been content to demonstrate the dependence of the terminology of relationship upon forms of marriage. In spending so much time upon this aspect of my subject I fear that I may have been helping to strengthen a very general misconception, for it is frequently supposed that the sole aim of those who think as I do is to explain systems of relationship by their origin in forms of marriage. Marriage is only one of the social institutions which have moulded the terminology of relationship. It is, however, so fundamental a social institution that it is difficult to get far away from it in any argument which deals with social organization. In now passing to other examples of the dependence of the terminology of relationship upon social conditions, I begin with one in which features of this terminology have come about, not as the result of forms of marriage, but of an attitude towards social regulations connected with marriage. The instance I have now to consider is closely allied to one which Professor Kroeber has used as his pattern of the psychological causation of the terminology of relationship.

Both in Polynesia and Melanesia it is not infrequent for the father-in-law to be classed with the father, the mother-in-law with the mother, the brother-in-law with the brother, and the sister-in-law with the sister. The Oceanic terminology of relationship has two features which enable us to study the exact nature of this process in more detail than is possible with our own system. Oceanic languages often distinguish carefully between different kinds of brother- and sister-in-law, and, if it be found that it is only certain kinds of brother- or sister-in-law who are classed with the brother or sister, we may thereby obtain a clue to the nature of the process whereby the classing has come about. Secondly, Oceanic terminology usually distinguishes relationships between men or between women from those between persons of different sex, and there is a feature of the terminology employed when brothers- or sisters-in-law are classed with brothers or sisters in Oceania which throws much light on the process whereby this common nomenclature has come into use.

The first point to be noticed in the Oceanic nomenclature of relationship is that not all brothers- and sisters-in-law are classed with brothers and sisters, but only those of different sex. Thus, in Merlav, in the Banks Islands, it is only the wife's sister and a man's brother's wife who are classed with the sister, and the husband's brother and a woman's sister's husband who are classed with the brother, while there are special terms for other categories of relative whom we include under the designations brother- and sister-in-law. Similar conditions are general throughout Melanesia. If, as Professor Kroeber has supposed, the classing of the brother-in-law with the brother be due to the psychological similarity of the relationships, we ought to be able to discover why this similarity should be greater between persons of different sex than between persons of the same sex.

If now we study our case from the Banks Islands more closely and compare the social conditions in Merlav with those of other islands of the group, we find definite evidence, which it will not now be possible to consider in detail, showing that sexual relations were formerly allowed between a man and his wife's sisters and his brother's wives, and that there is a definite association between the classing of these relatives with the sister and the cessation of such sexual relations. If such people as the Melanesians wish to emphasize in the strongest manner possible the impropriety of sexual relations between a man and the sisters of his wife, there is no way in which they can do it more effectually than by classing these relatives with a sister. To a Melanesian, as to other people of rude culture, the use of a term otherwise applied to a sister carries with it such deeply seated associations as to put sexual relations absolutely out of the question. There is a large body of evidence from southern Melanesia which suggests strongly, if not conclusively, that the common nomenclature I am now considering has arisen out of the social need for emphasizing the impropriety of relations which were once habitual among the people.

The second feature of Melanesian terminology which I have mentioned helps us to understand how the common nomenclature has come about. In most of the Melanesian cases in which a wife's sister is denoted by a term otherwise used for a sister, or a husband's brother by a term otherwise used for a brother, the term employed is one which is normally used between those of the same sex. Thus, a man does not apply to his wife's sister the term which he himself uses for his sister, but one which would be used by a woman of her sister. In other words, a man uses for his wife's sister the term which is used for this relative by his wife. This shows us how the common nomenclature may have come into use. It suggests that as sexual relations with the wife's sister became no longer orthodox, a man came to apply to this woman the word with which he was already familiar as a term for this relative from the mouth of his wife. The special feature of Melanesian nomenclature according to which terms of relationship vary with the sex of the speaker here helps us to understand how the common nomenclature arose. The process is one in which psychological factors evidently play an important part, but these psychological factors are themselves the outcome of a social process, viz., the change from a condition of sexual communism to one in which sexual relations are restricted to the partners of a marriage. Such psychological factors as come into action are only intermediate links in a chain of causation in which the two ends are definitely social processes or events, or, perhaps more correctly, psychological concomitants of intermediate links which are themselves social events. We should be shutting our eyes to obvious featusre of these Melanesian customs if we refused to recognize that the terminology of relationship here 'reflects' sociology.

This leads me to question for a moment whether it may not be the same with that custom of our own society which Professor Kroeber has taken as his example of the psychological causation of the terminology of relationship. Is it as certain as Professor Kroeber supposes that the classing of the brother-in-law with the brother, or of the sister-in-law with the sister, among ourselves does not reflect sociology? We know that there are social factors at work among us which give to these relationships, and especially to that of wife's sister, a very great importance. If instead of stating dogmatically that this feature of our own terminology is due to the psychological similarity of the relationships, Professor Kroeber's mind had been open even to the possibility of the working of social causes, I think he might have been led to inquire more closely into the distribution and exact character of the practice in question. He might have been led to see that we have here a problem for exact inquiry. Such a custom among ourselves must certainly own a cause different from that to which I have ascribed the Melanesian practice, but is it certain that there is no social practice among ourselves which would lead to the classing of the wife's sister with the sister and the sister's husband of a woman with the brother? I will only point to the practice of marrying the deceased wife's sister, and content myself with the remark that I should be surprised if there were any general tendency to class these relatives together by a people among whom this form of marriage is the orthodox and habitual custom.

Till now I have been dealing with relatively small variations of the classificatory system. The varieties I have so far considered are such as would arise out of a common system if in one place there came into vogue the cross-cousin marriage, in another place marriage with the wife of the mother's brother, in another that with the granddaughter of the brother or with the wife of the grandfather, and in yet other places combinations of these forms of marriage. I have now to consider whether it is possible to refer the main varieties of the classificatory system to social conditions; as an example with which to begin, I choose one which is so definite that it attracted the attention of Morgan, viz., the variety of the classificatory system which Morgan called 'Malayan'. It is now generally recognized that this term was badly chosen. The variety so called was known to Morgan through the terminology of the Hawaiian Islands, and as the system of these islands was not only the first to be recorded, but is also that of which even now we have the most complete record, I propose to use it as the pattern and to speak of the Hawaiian system where Morgan spoke of the Malayan. If now we compare the Hawaiian system with the forms of the classificatory system found in other parts of Oceania, in Australia, India, Africa or America, we find that it is characterized by its extreme simplicity and by the fewness of its terms. Distinctions such as those between the father's brother and the mother's brother, between the father's sister and the mother's sister, and between the children of brothers or of sisters and the children of brother and sister, distinctions which are so generally present in the more usual forms of the classificatory system, are here completely absent. The problem before us is to discover whether the absence of these distinctions can be referred to any social factors. If not, we may be driven to suppose that there is something in the structure of the Polynesian mind which leads the Hawaiian and the Maori to see similarities where most other peoples of rude culture see differences.

The first point to be noted is that in Oceania the distinction between the Hawaiian and the more usual forms of the classificatory system does not correspond with the distinction between the Polynesian and Melanesian peoples. Systems are to be found in Melanesia, as in the western Solomons, which closely resemble that of Hawaii, while there are Polynesian systems, such as those of Tonga and Tikopia, which are so like those of Melanesia that, if they had occurred there, they would have attracted no special attention. The difference between the two kinds of system is not to be correlated with any difference of race.

Next, if we take Melanesian and Polynesian systems as a whole, we find that they do not fall into two sharply marked-off groups, but that there are any number of intermediate gradations between the two. It would be possible to arrange the classificatory systems of Oceania in a series in which it would not be possible to draw the line at any point between the different varieties of system which the two ends of the series seem to represent. The question arises whether it is possible to find any other series of transitions in Oceania which runs parallel with the series connecting the two varieties of system of relationship. There is no doubt but that this question can be answered in the affirmative.

Speaking broadly, there are two main varieties of social organization in Oceania, with an infinite number of intermediate conditions. In one variety marriage is regulated by some kind of clan-exogamy, including under the term 'clan' the moieties of a dual organization; in the other variety marriage is regulated by kinship or genealogical relationship. We know of no part of Melanesia where marriage is regulated solely by clan-exogamy, but it is possible to arrange Melanesian and Polynesian societies in a series according to the different degrees in which the principles of genealogical relationship is the determining factor in the regulation of marriage. At one end of the series we should have places like the Banks Islands, the northern New Hebrides and the

Santa Cruz Islands, where the clan-organization is so obviously important that it was the only mechanism for the regulation of marriage which was recognized even by so skilful an observer as Dr Codrington. At the other end of the series we have places such as the Hawaiian Islands and Eddystone Island in the western Solomons, where only the barest traces of a clan-organization are to be found and where marriage is regulated solely by genealogical relationship. Between the two are numerous intermediate cases, and the series so formed runs so closely parallel to that representing the transitions between different forms of the classificatory system that it seems out of the question but that there should be a relation between the two. Of all the places where I have myself worked, the two in which I failed to find any trace of the regulation of marriage by means of a clan-organization were the Hawaiian Islands and Eddystone Island, and the systems of both places were lacking in just those distinctions the absence of which characterized the Malayan system of Morgan. Only in one point did the Eddystone system differ from the Hawaiian. Though the mother's brother was classed in nomenclature with the father, there was a term for the sister's son, but it was so little used that in a superficial survey it would have escaped notice. Its use was so exceptional that many of the islanders were doubtful about its proper meaning. In other parts of the Solomons where the clan-organization persists, but where the regulation of marriage by genealogical relationship is equally, if not more, important, the systems of relationship show intermediate characters. Thus, in the island of Florida the mother's brother was distinguished from the father and there was a term by means of which to distinguish cross-cousins from other kinds of cousin, but the father's sister was classed with the mother, and it was habitual to ignore the proper term for cross-cousins and to class them in nomenclature with brothers and sisters and with cousins of other kinds, as in the Hawaiian system. One influential man even applied the term for father to the mother's brother; it was evident that a change is even now in progress which would have to go very little farther to make the Florida system indistinguishable in structure from that of Hawaii.

Among the western Papuo-Melanesians of New Guinea, again, the systems of relationship come very near to the Hawaiian type, and with this character there is associated a very high degree of

importance of the regulation of marriage by genealogical relationship and a vagueness of clan-organization. We have here so
close a parallelism between two series of social phenomena as to
supply as good an example as could be wished of the application of the method of concomitant variations in the domain of
sociology.

The nature of these changes and their relation to the general
cultures of the peoples who use the different forms of terminology
show that the transitions are to be associated with a progressive
change which has taken place in Oceania. In this part of the world
the classificatory system has been the seat of a process of simplifica-
tion starting from the almost incredible complexity of Pentecost
and reaching the simplicity of such systems as those of Eddystone
or Mekeo. This process has gone hand in hand with one in which
the regulation of marriage by some kind of clan-exogamy has
gradually been replaced by a mechanism based on relationship as
traced by means of pedigrees.

If this conclusion be accepted, it will follow that the more
widely distributed varieties of the classificatory system of relationship are associated with a social structure which has the exogamous social group as its essential unit. This position has only
to be stated for it to become apparent how all the main features
of the classificatory system are such as would follow directly
from such a social structure. Whenever the classificatory system is
found in association with a system of exogamous social groups,
the terms of relationship do not apply merely to relatives with
whom it is possible to trace genealogical relationship, but to all
the members of a clan of a given generation, even if no such relationship with them can be traced. Thus, a man will not only
apply the term 'father' to all the brothers of his father, to all the
sons' sons of his father's father, and to all the sons' sons' sons of his
father's father's father, to all the husbands of his mother's sisters
and of his mother's mother's granddaughters, etc., but he will
also apply the term to all the members of his father's clan of the
same generation as his father and to all the husbands of the women
of the mother's clan of the same generation as the mother, even
when it is quite impossible to show any genealogical relationship
with them. All these and the other main features of the classificatory system become at once natural and intelligible if this
system had its origin in a social structure in which exogamous

social groups, such as the clan or moiety, were even more completely and essentially the social units than we know them to be today among the peoples whose social systems have been carefully studied. If you are dissatisfied with the word 'classificatory' as a term for the system of relationship which is found in America, Africa, India, Australia and Oceania, you would be perfectly safe in calling it the 'clan' system, and in inferring the ancient presence of a social structure based on the exogamous clan even if this structure were no longer present.

Not only is the general character of the classificatory system exactly such as would be the consequence of its origin in a social structure founded on the exogamous social group, but many details of these systems point in the same direction. Thus, the rigorous distinctions between father's brother and mother's brother, and between father's sister and mother's sister, which are characteristic of the usual forms of the classificatory system, are the obvious consequence of the principle of exogamy. If this principle be in action, these relatives must always belong to different social groups, so that it would be natural to distinguish them in nomenclature.

Further, there are certain features of the classificatory system which suggest its origin in a special form of exogamous social grouping, viz., that usually known as the dual system in which there are only two social groups or moieties. It is an almost universal feature of the classificatory system that the children of brothers are classed with the children of sisters. A man applies the same term to his mother's sister's children which he uses for his father's brother's children, and the use of this term, being the same as that used for a brother or sister, carries with it the most rigorous prohibition of marriage. Such a condition would not follow necessarily from a social state in which there were more than two social groups. If the society were patrilineal, the children of two brothers would necessarily belong to the same social group, so that the principle of exogamy would prevent marriage between them, but if the women of the group had married into different clans, there is no reason arising out of the principle of exogamy which should prevent marriage between their children or lead to the use of a term common to them and the children of brothers. Similarly, if the society were matrilineal, the children of two sisters would necessarily belong to the same social group, but this would not be the case with the children of brothers who might marry into different social groups.

If, however, there be only two social groups, the case is very different. It would make no difference whether descent were patrilineal or matrilineal. In each case the children of two brothers or of two sisters must belong to the same moiety, while the children of brother and sister must belong to different moieties. The children of two brothers would be just as ineligible as consorts as the children of two sisters. Similarly, it would be a natural consequence of the dual organization that the mother's brother's children should be classed with the father's sister's children, but this would not be necessary if there were more than two social groups.

I should have liked, if there were time, to deal with other features of the classificatory system, but must be content with these examples. I hope to have succeeded in showing that the social causation of the terminology of relationship goes far beyond the mere dependence of features of the system on special forms of marriage, and that the character of the classificatory system as a whole has been determined by its origin in a specific form of social organization. I propose now to leave the classificatory system for a moment and inquire whether another system of denoting and classifying relationships may not similarly be shown to be determined by social conditions. The system I shall consider is our own. Let us examine this system in its relation to the form of social organization prevalent among ourselves.

Just as among most peoples of rude culture the clan or other exogamous group is the essential unit of social organization, so among ourselves this social unit is the family, using this term for the group consisting of a man, his wife, and their children. If we examine our terms of relationship, we find that those applied to individual persons and those used in a narrow and well-defined sense are just those in which the family is intimately concerned. The terms father, mother, husband and wife, brother and sister, are limited to members of the family of the speaker, and the terms father-, mother-, brother-, and sister-in-law to the members of the family of the wife or husband in the same narrowly restricted sense. Similarly, the terms grandfather and grandmother are limited to the parents of the father and mother, while the terms grandson and granddaughter are only used of the families of the children in the narrow sense. The terms uncle and aunt, nephew and niece, are used in a less restricted sense, but even these terms are only used of persons who stand in a close relation to the family of the speaker. We have only one term used with anything approaching the wide connotation of classificatory terms of relationship, and this term is used for a group of relatives who have as their chief feature in common that they are altogether outside the proper circle of the family and have no social obligations or privileges. They are as eligible for marriage as any other members of the community, and only in the very special cases I considered in the first lecture are they brought into any kind of legal relation. The dependence of our own use of terms of relationship on the social institution of the family seems to me so obvious that I find it difficult to understand how anyone who has considered these terms can put forward the view that the terminology of relationship is not socially conditioned. It seems to me that we have only to have the proposition stated that the classificatory system and our own are the outcome of the social institutions of the clan and family respectively for the social causation of such terminology to become conspicuous. I find it difficult to understand why it has not long before this been universally recognized. I do not think we can have a better example of the confusion and prejudice which have been allowed to envelop the subject through the unfortunate introduction of the problem of the primitive promiscuity or monogamy of mankind. It is not necessary to have an expert knowledge of the classificatory system. It is only necessary to consider the terms we have used almost from our cradles in relation to their social setting to see how the terminology of relationship has been determined by that setting.

This brief study of our own terms of relationship leads me to speak about the name by which our system is generally known. Morgan called it the 'descriptive system', and this term has been generally adopted. I believe, however, that it is wholly inappropriate. Those terms which apply to one person and to one person only may be called descriptive if you please, though even here the use does not seem very happy. When we pass beyond these, however, our terms are no whit more descriptive than those of the classificatory system. We speak of a grandfather, not of a father's father or a mother's father, only distinguishing grandfathers in this manner when it is necessary to supplement our customary terminology by more exact description. Similarly, we speak of a brother-in-law, and only in exceptional circumstances do we use forms of language which indicate whether reference is being made to the brother of the husband or wife or to the husband of a sister. Such occasional usages do not make our system descriptive, and if they be held to do so, the classificatory system is just as descriptive as our own. All those peoples who use the classificatory system are capable of such exact description of relationship as I have mentioned. Indeed, classificatory systems are often more descriptive than our own. In some forms of this system true descriptive terms are found in habitual use. Thus, in the coastal systems of Fiji the mother's brother is often called *ngandina* (*ngane*, sister of a man, and *tina*, mother), this term being used in place of the *vungo* already mentioned. Similar uses of descriptive terms occur in other parts of Melanesia. Thus, in Santa Cruz the father's sister is called *inwerderde* (*inwe*, sister, and *derde*, father). This relative is one for whom Melanesian systems of relationship not infrequently possess no special designation, and the use of a descriptive term suggests a recent process which has come into action in order to denote a relative who had previously lacked any special designation.

If 'descriptive' is thus an inappropriate name for our own system, it will be necessary to find another, and I should like boldly to recognize the direct dependence of its characters on the institution of the family and to speak of it as the 'family system'.

While I thus reject the term 'descriptive' as a proper name for the terminology of relationship with which we are especially familiar, it does not follow that there may not be systems of denoting relationship which properly deserve this title. In Samoa a mode of denoting relatives is often used in which the great majority of the terms are descriptive. Thus, the only term which I could obtain for the father's brother's son was *atalii o le uso o le tama*, which is literally 'son of the brother of the father', and there is some reason to suppose that this descriptive usage has come into vogue owing to the total inadequacy of the ancient Samoan system to express relationships in which the peoples are now interested.

The wide use of such descriptive terms is also found in many systems of Europe, as in the Celtic languages, in those of

Scandinavia, in Lithuanian and Estonian.[1] A similar mode of denoting relationships is found in Semitic languages and among the Shilluk and Dinka of the Sudan, and since it is from these peoples that I have gained my own experience of descriptive terminology, I propose to take them as my examples.

In the Arabic system of relationship used in Egypt many of the terms are descriptive; thus, the father's brother being called '*amm*, the father's brother's wife is *mirat 'ammi*, the father's brother's son *ibn 'ammi*, and the father's brother's daughter *bint 'ammi*, and there is a similar usage for the consorts and children of the father's sister and of the brother and sister of the mother.

Similarly, many Shilluk terms suggest a descriptive character, the father's brother being *wa*, the wife of the father's brother is *chiwa*, the father's brother's son is *uwa*, and his daughter is *nyuwa*. The father's sister being *waja*, her son and daughter are *uwaja* and *nyuwaja* respectively. Similar descriptive terms are used by the Dinka. The father's brother being *walen*, the father's brother's son is *manwalen* and his daughter *yanwalen*; the mother's brother being *ninar*, the mother's brother's son is *manninar* and his daughter *yanninar*.

According to the main thesis of these lectures, these descriptive usages should own some definite social cause. The descriptive terminology seems to be particularly definite in the case of cousins, and it might be suggested that they are dependent, at any rate in part and in so far as Egypt is concerned, on the prevalence of marriage with a cousin. Marriages with the daughter of a father's brother or of a mother's brother are especially orthodox and popular in Egypt, and different degrees of preference for marriage with different classes of cousin would produce just such a social need as would have led to the definite distinction of the different kinds of cousin from one another by means of descriptive terms.

It is more probable, however, that the use of descriptive terms in the languages of the Semites and of the Shilluk and Dinka has been the outcome of a definite form of social organization, viz., that in which the social unit is neither the family in the narrow sense, nor the clan, but that body of persons of common descent living in one house or in some other kind of close association which we call the patriarchal or extended family, the *Gross-*

---

[1] See Tables in Morgan's *Systems . . .*, pp. 79–127.

familie of the Germans. It is a feature of the Semitic and Nilotic systems, not only to distinguish the four chief categories of cousin, but also the four chief kinds of uncle or aunt, viz., the father's brother, the father's sister, the mother's brother and the mother's sister, all of whom are habitually classed together in our system, while some of them are classed with the father or mother in the classificatory system. The Semitic and Nilotic terminology is such as would follow from a form of social organization in which the more intimate relationships of the family in the narrow sense are definitely recognized, but yet certain uncles, aunts, and cousins are of so much importance as to make it necessary for social purposes that they shall be denoted exactly. The brothers of the father and the unmarried sisters of the father would be of the same social group as the father, while the brothers and unmarried sisters of the mother would be of a different social group, which would account for their distinctive nomenclature, while within the social group it would be necessary to distinguish the father from his brothers. It would be too cumbrous to call this variety of system after the extended family, and I suggest that it should be called the 'kindred' system.

Analogy with other parts of the world suggests that all those of the same generation in the social group formed by the extended family may once have been classed together under one term, and that, as later there arose social motives requiring the distinction of different relatives so classed together, descriptive terms came into use to make the necessary distinctions. You must please regard this only as a suggestion. We need far more detailed evidence concerning the social status of different relatives among the peoples who use these descriptive terms. Such knowledge as we possess seems to point to the dependence of the Semitic and Sudanese terminology upon the social institution of the extended family, just as our own system depends on the social institution of the family in the narrow sense and the classificatory system upon the clan.

If this descriptive mode of nomenclature be thus the outcome of a social organization of which the essential element is the extended family, I need hardly point out how natural it is that we should find this kind of nomenclature so widely in Europe. The presence of this descriptive terminology in Celtic and Scandinavian languages, in Lithuanian and Estonian, would be examples of the persistence of a form of nomenclature which had its origin in the kindred of the extended family. On this view we must believe that, in other languages of Europe, this mode of nomenclature has gradually been replaced by one dependent on the social institution of the family in the narrow sense.

At this point I should like to sum up briefly the position to which our argument has taken us. I have first shown the dependence of a number of special features of the classificatory system of relationship upon special forms of marriage. Then I have shown that certain broad varieties of the classificatory system are to be referred to different forms of social organization and to the different degrees in which the regulation of marriage by means of clan-exogamy has been replaced by a mechanism dependent upon kinship or genealogical relationship. From that I was led to refer the general features of the classificatory system to the dependence of this system upon the social unit of the clan as opposed to the family which I believe to be the basis of our own terminology of relationship. I then pointed to several features of the classificatory system which suggest that it arose in that special variety of the clan-organization in which a community consists of two exogamous moieties, forming the social structure usually known as the dual organization. I considered more fully the dependence of our own mode of denoting relatives upon the social institution of the family, and then a study of the descriptive terminology of relationship has led me to suggest that certain modes of denoting relationship in Egypt, the Sudan and many European countries may be examples of a third main variety of system of relationship which has arisen out of the patriarchal or extended family. We should thus have three main varieties of system of relationship in place of the two which have hitherto been recognized, having their origins respectively in the clan, in the family in the narrow sense and in the extended or patriarchal family. These three varieties may be regarded as genera within each of which are species and varieties depending upon special social conditions which have arisen within each kind of social grouping, either as the result of changes within each form of social organization or of transitions from one form to another. We know of a far larger number of such varieties within the classificatory system than within those due to the two forms of the family, and this is probably due in some measure to the fact that the classificatory system is still by far the most widely distributed form over the earth's surface. Still more important, however, is the fact that among the peoples who use the classificatory system there is an infinitely greater variety of social institution, and especially of forms of marriage, than exist among civilized peoples whose main social unit, the family, is not one which is capable of any extended range of variation. The result of the complete survey has been to justify my use of the classificatory system as the means whereby to demonstrate the dependence of the terminology of relationship upon social conditions. It is the great variability of this mode of denoting relatives which makes it so valuable an instrument for the study of the laws which have governed the history of that department of language by which mankind has denoted those who stand in social relations to himself.

You may have been wondering whether I am going to say anything about the merits of the controversy which has till now given to systems of relationship their chief interest among students of sociology. I have so far left on one side the subjects which have been the main ground of controversy ever since the time of Morgan. You will have gathered that I regard it as a grave misfortune for the science of sociology that the topics of promiscuity and group-marriage should have been thrust by Morgan into the prominent place which they have ever since occupied in the theoretical study of relationship. Even now I should have liked to leave them on one side on the ground that the evidence is as yet insufficient to make them profitable subjects for such exact inquiry as I believe to be the proper business of sociology. Their very prominence, however, makes it impossible to leave them wholly unconsidered, but I propose to deal with them very briefly.

I begin with the question whether the classificatory system of relationship provides us with any evidence that mankind once possessed a form of social organization, or rather such an absence of social organization, as would accompany a condition of general promiscuity in which, if one can speak of marriage at all, marriage was practised between all and any members of the community, including brothers and sisters. I can deal with this subject very briefly because I hope to have succeeded elsewhere in knocking away the support on which the whole of Morgan's own construction rested.

Morgan deduced his stage of promiscuity from the Hawaiian system, which he supposed to be the most primitive form of classificatory nomenclature. In an article published in 1907 I showed[1] that it rather represents a late stage in the history of the more ordinary forms of the classificatory system. My conclusion at that time was based on the scanty evidence derived from the relatively few Oceanic systems which had then been recorded, but my work since that article was written has shown the absolute correctness of my earlier opinion, which I can now support by a far larger body of evidence than was available in 1907. It remains possible, however, that the Hawaiian system may have had its source in promiscuity, even though this condition be late rather than primitive, but it would be going beyond the scope of these lectures to deal fully with this subject here. I cannot forbear, however, from mentioning that Hawaiian promiscuity, in so far as it existed, was not the condition of the whole people, but only of the chiefs who alone were allowed to contract brother and sister marriages, while I have evidence that the avoidance of brother and sister in Melanesia, which has so often been regarded as a survival of man's early promiscuity, is capable of a very different explanation.[2] Our available knowledge, whether derived from features of the classificatory system or from other social facts, does not provide one shred of evidence in favour of such a condition as was put forward by Morgan as the earliest stage of human society, nor is there any evidence that such promiscuity has ever been the ruling principle of a people at any later stage of the history of mankind.

The subject of group-marriage is one about which I do not find it possible to speak so dogmatically. It would take me more than another lecture to deal adequately with the Melanesian evidence alone, and I must content myself with two remarks. Firstly, I think it desirable to throw aside the term group-marriage as only confusing the issue, and to speak rather of a state of organized sexual communism, in which sexual relations are recognized as orthodox between the men of one social group and

---

[1] *Anthropological Essays presented to E. B. Tylor*, Oxford, 1907, p. 309.

[2] For the full evidence on these topics see my forthcoming book, *The History of Melanesian Society*.

the women of another. Secondly, the classificatory system has several features which would follow naturally from such a condition of sexual communism. I have evidence from Melanesia which places beyond question the former presence of such a condition, with features of culture which become readily explicable if they be the survivals of such a state of sexual communism as is suggested by the terminology of the classificatory system. This evidence comes from only one part of the world, but it is enough to convince me that we have no right to dismiss from our minds a state of organized sexual communism as a feature of the social development of mankind. The wide distribution of the classificatory system would suggest that this communism has been very general, but it need not have been universal, and even if the widespread existence of organized sexual communism be established, it would not follow that it represents the earliest stage in the evolution of human society. There are certain features even of the classificatory system itself which suggest that, if this system be founded in sexual communism, this communism was not primitive, but grew out of a condition in which only such ties of kinship were recognized as would result from the social institution of the family.

I must be content with this brief reference to the subject. The object of these lectures is to demonstrate the dependence of the terminology of relationship upon social conditions, and the dependence of the classificatory system upon a condition of sexual communism is not now capable of demonstration. The classificatory mode of denoting relationship should, however, act as a suggestion and stimulus, and as a preventative of dogmatic statement in a part of our subject which, in spite of its entrancing interest, still lies only at the edge of our slowly spreading circle of exact knowledge.

In conclusion, I should like to point out briefly some of the lessons of more general interest which may be learnt from the facts I have brought before you in these lectures. I hope that one result has been to convince you of the danger lying in the use of the *reductio ad absurdum* argument when dealing with cultures widely different from our own. In the literature of the subject one often meets the adjectives 'absurd' and 'impossible' applied in some cases to social conditions in which the actual existence of the absurdities or impossibilities can be demonstrated. I may take as

G

an example the argument of Mr N. W. Thomas, which I have already mentioned, in which the classing of the maternal grandfather with the elder brother by the Dieri is regarded as reducing to an absurdity the contention that classificatory terms express ties of kinship. If Mr Thomas had had a more lively faith in the social meaning of terms of relationship, he might have been led to notice that the Dieri marry the granddaughter of a brother, a fact he appears, in common with many other readers of Howitt, to have missed; one result of this marriage is to bring about just such a relationship as Howitt records without a man being his own great-uncle, as is supposed to be necessary by Mr Thomas.

Still another example may be taken from Professor Kroeber. He states that the classing together of the grandfather and the father-in-law which is found in the Dakota system, when worked out to its implications, would lead to the absurd conclusion that marriage with the mother was once customary among the Sioux. Here again, if Professor Kroeber had been less imbued with his belief in a purely linguistic and psychological chain of causation, and had been ready to entertain the idea that there might be a social meaning, he must have been led to see that the features of nomenclature in question would follow from other forms of marriage, and two of these, whatever their apparent improbability in America, cannot well be called absurd, since they are known to occur in other parts of the world. Following Riggs, Professor Kroeber does not specify which kinds of grandfather and father-in-law are classed together in Dakota nomenclature, but in the full list given by Morgan, it is evident that one term is used for the fathers of both father and mother and for the fathers of both husband and wife. The classing of the father's father with the wife's father would be a natural result of marriage with the father's sister, while the common nomenclature for father's father and husband's father would result from marriage with the brother's daughter. It is not without significance that the features of nomenclature which would be the result of one or other, or of both these marriages, occur in a system which also bears evidence of the cross-cousin marriage, for these three forms of marriage occur in conjunction in one part of Melanesia, viz., the Torres Islands.

The foregoing instance, together with many others scattered through these lectures, will have pointed clearly to another lesson.

In the present state of our knowledge a working scheme or hypothesis has largely to be judged by its utility. A way of regarding social phenomena which obstructs inquiry and leads people to overlook facts has its disadvantages, to say the least, while a scheme or hypothesis which leads people to worry out and discover things which do not lie on the surface will establish a strong claim on our consideration, even if it should ultimately turn out to be only the partial truth. I will give only one instance to illustrate how a belief in the dependence of the terminology of relationship on forms of marriage might act as a stimulus to research.

In a system from the United Provinces recorded by Mr E. A. H. Blunt in the Report of the last Indian Census, one term, *bahu*, is used for the son's wife, for the wife, and for the mother.[1] Mr Blunt puts on one side without hesitation the possibility that such common nomenclature can have been the result of any form of marriage, and ascribes it to the custom whereby a man and his wife live with the husband's parents, in consequence of which the son's wife, who is called *bahu* by her husband, is also called *bahu* by everyone else in the house. The causation of the common nomenclature which is thus put forward is a possible, perhaps even a probable, explanation. In such a case we should have a social chain of causation in which the son's wife is called *bahu* because she is one of a social group bound together by the ties of a common habitation. It can do no harm, however, to bear in mind as an alternative the possibility that the terminology may have arisen out of a form of marriage. It is evident that the use of a common term for the wife and the son's wife would follow from a form of polyandry in which a man and his son have a wife in common. A further result of this form of marriage would be that the wife of the son, being also the wife of his father, would have the status of a mother.[2] We have no evidence for the presence of such a marriage in India, but our knowledge of the sociology of the more backward peoples of India is not so complete that we can afford to neglect any clue. The possibility suggested by the mode of using the term *bahu* should lead us to look for other evidence of such a form of polyandry among the ruder

[1] *Census of India*, 1911, vol. xv, p. 234.
[2] In such a case the use of the term by other members of the household, including women, would be the result of a later extension of meaning.

elements of the population of India, of whose social structure our present knowledge is so fragmentary.

Another important result of our study of the terminology of relationship is that it helps us to understand the proper place of psychological explanation in sociology. These lectures have largely been devoted to the demonstration of the failure to explain features of the terminology of relationship on psychological grounds. If this demonstration has been successful, it is not because the terminology of relationship is anything peculiar, differing from other bodies of sociological facts; it is because in relationship we have to do with definite and clean-cut facts. The terminology of relationship is only a specially favourable example by means of which to show the value of an attitude towards, and mode of treatment of, social facts which hold good, though less conspicuously, throughout the whole field of sociology.

In social, as in all other kinds of human activity, psychological factors must have an essential part. I have myself in these lectures pointed to psychological considerations as elements in the problems with which the sociologist has to deal. These psychological elements are, however, only concomitants of social processes with which it is possible to deal apart from their psychological aspect. It has been the task of these lectures to refer the social facts of relationship to antecedent social conditions, and I believe that this is the proper method of sociology. Even at the present time, however, it is possible to support sociological arguments by means of considerations provided by psychological motives, and the assistance thus rendered to sociology will become far greater as the science of social psychology advances.

This is, however, a process very different from the interpolation of psychological facts as links in the chain of causation connecting social antecedents with social consequences. It is in no spirit of hostility to social psychology, but in the hope that it may help us to understand its proper place in the study of social institutions that I venture to put forward the method followed in these lectures as one proper to the science of sociology.[1]

It may be that there will be those who will accept my main position, but will urge that these lectures have been devoted to the

[1] See also 'Survival in Sociology', *Sociological Review*, 1913, vol. VI, p. 293. I hope shortly to deal more fully with the relations between sociology and social psychology.

criticism of an extreme position, the position taken up by Professor Kroeber. They may say that they have never believed in the purely psychological causation of the terminology of relationship. In reply to such an attitude I can only express my conviction that the paper of Professor Kroeber is only the explicit and clear statement of an attitude which is implicit in the work of nearly all, if not all, the opponents of Morgan since McLennan. Whether they have themselves recognized it or not, I believe that it has been this underlying attitude towards sociological problems which has prevented them from seeing what is good in Morgan's work, from sifting out the chaff from the wheat of his argument, and from recognizing how great is the importance to the science of sociology of the body of facts which Morgan was the first to collect and study. I feel that we owe a debt of gratitude to Professor Kroeber for having brought the matter into the open and for having presented, as a clear issue, a fundamental problem of the methods of sociology.

Lastly, I should like to point out how rigorous and exact has been the process of the determination of the nomenclature of relationship by social conditions which has been demonstrated in these lectures. We have here a case in which the principle of determinism applies with a rigour and definiteness equal to that of any of the exact sciences. According to my scheme, not only has the general character of systems of relationship been strictly determined by social conditions, but every detail of these systems has also been so determined. Even so small and apparently insignificant a feature as the classing of the sister-in-law with the sister has been found to lead back to a definite social condition arising out of the regulation of marriage and of sexual relations. If sociology is to become a science fit to rank with other sciences, it must, like them, be rigorously deterministic. Social phenomena do not come into being of themselves. The proposition that we class two relatives together in nomenclature because the relationships are similar is, if it stand alone, nothing more than a form of words. It is incumbent on those who believe in the importance of the psychological similarity of social phenomena to show in what the supposed similarity consists and how it has come about—in other words, how it has been determined. It has been my chief object in these lectures to show that, in so far as such similarities exist in the case of relationship, they have been determined by social conditions. Only by attention to this aim throughout the whole field of social phenomena can we hope to rid sociology of the reproach, so often heard, that it is not a science; only thus can we refute those who go still further and claim that it can never be a science.

The Genealogical Method of Anthropological Inquiry*

It is a familiar fact that many peoples preserve long pedigrees of their ancestors, going back for many generations and often shading off into the mythical. It is perhaps not so well known that most people of low culture preserve orally their pedigrees for several generations in all the collateral lines so that they can give in genealogical form all the descendants of the great-grandfather or of the great-great-grandfather and therefore know fully all those whom we should call second or third cousins and sometimes their memories go even farther back. It is this latter kind of genealogy which is used in the method I propose to consider in this paper.

I begin with the method of collecting the pedigrees which furnish the basis of the method. The first point to be attended to is that, owing to the great difference between the systems of relationship of savage and civilized peoples, it is desirable to use as few terms denoting kinship as possible, and complete pedigrees can be obtained when the terms are limited to the following: father, mother, child, husband and wife. The small pedigree which is given as a sample was obtained in Guadalcanal in the Eastern Solomon Islands, and in this case I began the inquiry by asking my informant, Kurka or Arthur, the name of his father and mother, making it clear that I wanted the names of his real parents and not of any other people whom he would call such by virtue of the classificatory system of relationship. After ascertaining that Kulini had had only one wife and Kusua only one husband, I obtained the names of their children in order of age and inquired into the marriages and offspring of each. Thus was obtained the small group consisting of the descendants of Arthur's parents. Guadalcanal being an island whose social system is characterized

* Reprinted from *The Sociological Review*, vol. 3, pp. 1–12, Jan. 1910.

by matrilineal descent, Arthur knew the pedigree of his mother better than that of his father. I obtained the names of her parents, ascertaining as before that each had only been once married, and then asked the names of their children and obtained the marriages and descendants of each. Arthur was a man who had been away for a long time in Queensland and was not able to go beyond his grandparents, but if he had had more extensive knowledge, I

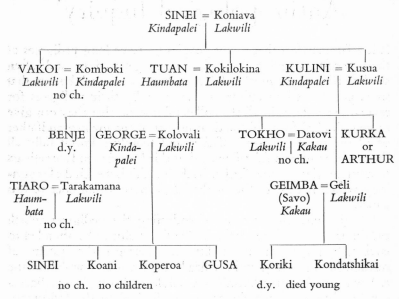

should have inquired into the parentage of Sinei and Koniava, and obtained the descendants of their parents in exactly the same manner, and should proceed till the genealogical knowledge of his family possessed by my informant was completely exhausted. In collecting the pedigrees the descendants in both the male and female lines are obtained, but in writing them out in order to use them for the purposes to be considered in this paper, it is well to record on one sheet only the descendants in one line with cross-references to other sheets for the descendants in the other line.[1] The exact method of arranging the names is a matter of no

---

[1] For the method of arrangement of a large mass of genealogical material the reader must be referred to *The Todas*, London, 1906, and the *Reports of the Cambridge Expedition to Torres Straits*, vols. v and vi.

great importance, but I have found it convenient to record the names of males in capital letters and those of females in ordinary type, and I always put the name of the husband to the left of that of the wife. In polygynous or polyandrous marriages I include the names of the wives or husbands in square brackets.

A most important feature of the method is to record as far as possible the social condition of each person included in the pedigrees. The locality to which each person belongs should be obtained, and often it is necessary to record not only the district but also the name of some smaller territorial group, whether village or hamlet. If the people have a totemic organization, the names of the totem or totems of each person should be recorded, or if there are non-totemic clans or other social divisions, these should be given in the same way. In the sample pedigree from Guadalcanal the names under those of the persons refer to exogamous clans which probably have a totemic nature.[1]

In beginning work in a new place it is well to record any other facts about each person which may possibly have any social significance, and later the inquiry can be limited to those which are found to be important. Especial care should be taken to record the localities of those who have married into the community from other tribes or places. If adoption exists, the adopted children will almost certainly be included among those given as real children unless especial attention is devoted to the point, and in cases where it is possible, both real and adoptive parentage should be recorded.

In this collection of the material for the application of the genealogical method difficulties and sources of error are often encountered. One difficulty which I have met is the existence of a taboo on the names of the dead, and this can sometimes only be overcome with difficulty. In my own experience I have been compelled in consequence of this taboo to obtain the pedigrees in secret and from persons not of the family in question. Other sources of error and confusion are the practices of adoption and of exchanging names, and doubtless new sources of difficulty may be found by those who seek to obtain pedigrees in new places.

In order that the pedigrees may be used in the ways I propose to describe it is necessary to be satisfied that they are trustworthy. In collecting the pedigrees of a whole community, there will be

[1] See *Journ. Roy. Anth. Inst.*, 1909, vol. XXXIX, p. 156.

much overlapping; people who belong to the paternal stock of one informant will come in the maternal stock of another, and in the wife's ancestry of a third, and there will thus be ample opportunity of testing the agreement of the accounts of different informants. In nearly every community in which I have worked I have found that there are people with especial genealogical knowledge, and it is well to make use of these as much as possible. In my experience it is very dangerous to trust to young men, who nearly everywhere are no longer taking the trouble to learn the pedigrees from their elders, but if obtained from the latter, I have always found the pedigrees to be extraordinarily accurate when tested by the agreement of different accounts and by the general coherence of the complete genealogical record of the community.

Having now briefly described the method of recording the pedigrees and guaranteeing their accuracy I can proceed to detail the uses to which they may be put.

The first and most obvious use is in working out the systems of relationship. In nearly all people of the lower culture these differ so widely from our own that there is the greatest danger of falling into error if one merely attempts to obtain the equivalents of our own terms by the ordinary method of question and answer. My procedure is to ask my informant the terms which he would apply to the different members of his pedigree, and reciprocally the terms which they would apply to him. Thus in the case of the pedigree from Guadalcanal which I have given as a sample, I asked Arthur what he called Tokho which gave the equivalent of 'elder brother' when a man is speaking, while the name given by Tokho to Arthur gave the corresponding equivalent of 'younger brother'. The terms applied to one another by Vakoi and Arthur gave the equivalents of sister's son and mother's brother respectively, and the relationship of Komboki to Arthur gave the terms for mother's brother's wife and husband's sister's son, and the other relationships on the mother's side were obtained in the same manner. For the names of relationships on the father's side the pedigree of Kulini, Arthur's father, would be used. It is as a matter of fact only exceptionally that a complete set of terms of relationship can be obtained from a single pedigree, but even if this were possible it is not advisable to do so, for there is always the chance of the occurrence of some double relationship, perhaps one by consanguinity and another by marriage, which may mislead, and I am never wholly content with a kin-ship system unless each of the relationships has been obtained from three separate pedigrees.

The following list of terms of relationship should be obtained:

Father ⎫	son
Mother ⎭	daughter
Elder brother (m.s.)	younger brother (m.s.)
Elder brother (w.s.)	younger sister (m.s.)
Elder sister (m.s.)	younger brother (w.s.)
Elder sister (w.s.)	younger sister (w.s.)
Father's brother	brother's child (m.s.)
Father's brother's wife	husband's brother's child
Father's brother's child	
Father's sister	brother's child (w.s.)
Father's sister's husband	wife's brother's child
Father's sister's child	
Mother's brother	sister's child (m.s.)
Mother's brother's wife	husband's sister's child
Mother's brother's child	
Mother's sister	sister's child (w.s.)
Mother's sister's husband	wife's sister's child
Mother's sister's child	
Father's father	son's child (m.s.)
Father's mother	son's child (w.s.)
Mother's father	daughter's child (m.s.)
Mother's mother	daughter's child (w.s.)
Husband	wife
Wife's father	daughter's husband (m.s.)
Wife's mother	daughter's husband (w.s.)
Husband's father	son's wife (m.s.)
Husband's mother	son's wife (w.s.)
Wife's brother	sister's husband (m.s.)
Wife's sister	sister's husband (w.s.)
Husband's brother	brother's wife (m.s.)
Husband's sister	brother's wife (w.s.)
Wife's sister's husband	
Husband's brother's wife	
Son's wife's parents	

m.s.   man speaking   w.s.   woman speaking

They are arranged in two columns, those opposite to one another being reciprocals, so that if the terms are obtained by the genealogical method the name given by a man to any given relative would be entered in one column and the name given by the relative to him would have its place opposite to it. In the case

of many relationships two forms are used, one when addressing a
relative and the other when speaking of him, and both of these
should be obtained. In many parts of the world different terms
of relationship are used by people of different sexes, and the terms
are also affected by the respective ages of the two parties to the
relationship. In the list all the important differences according to
sex have been included by specifying whether the term is being
used by a man (m.s.) or a woman (w.s.), but the age-distinctions
have only been given in the cases of brothers and sisters. If, as
often happens, elder and younger brothers of the father are
distinguished these terms should also be obtained, and similar
distinctions should be inquired into in the case of other relationships. Sometimes the distinctions according to age go even
further, and there may be a distinctive term for each member of a
family of three, four, five or more. If sons are distinguished from
daughters in nomenclature, the terms should be given in each case
in the list where the word 'child' occurs.

The terms used for definite relationships by blood or marriage
are also often applied to others with whom no such ties can be
traced. I am in the habit of supplementing the genealogical
method by asking for a list of all the people to whom a given man
applies a term of relationship. On analysis it will usually be
found that these fall into four classes: (1) relationships which can
be traced in the pedigrees; (2) relationships by blood or marriage
which cannot be so traced in the pedigrees available but which
have nevertheless a genealogical basis, thus, in connection with
the sample pedigree Arthur might say that he called a man
nianggu or 'my mother's brother', because he was the *tasina* or
'brother' of Kusua; (3) relationships dependent on membership
of a social division, thus Arthur might call a man *kukuanggu* or
'my grandfather' because the latter was a Lakwili man of the
same generation as Koniava; (4) relationships dependent on some
artificial tie set up by the user of the term or even by his father or
grandfather, such artificial relationships being sometimes trans-
mitted from father to son.

The terms given in the list are sufficient to determine the
general character of a system, but it will be well to obtain a certain
number of terms for more distant relationships such as the father's
father's brother and sister together with their children and grandchildren. Among these more distant relationships the sister's

son's wife and sister's daughter's husband and their children are sometimes of special interest.

The next use of the pedigrees is in the study of the regulation of marriage. If the pedigrees of the whole of a population are collected as I have been able to do in several cases, we have in them a register of the marriages which have taken place in the community, reaching back perhaps for a hundred and fifty years. This register is preserved in the minds of the people and by its means we are able to study the laws regulating marriage just as in a civilized community one can make use of the records of a marriage registry office. We can see not only what marriages have been allowed or enjoined and what marriages have been prohibited, but we can express statistically the frequency of the different kinds. In many peoples of low culture there seems to be in progress a gradual transition from a condition in which marriage is regulated chiefly or entirely by means of a mechanism of clans or phratries or other social grouping to one in which the regulation of marriage depends on actual consanguinity, and the exact nature of the transitional stage of any given people can only be satisfactorily determined by such a concrete method as is provided by the study of a genealogical record. Further where marriage is regulated mainly by some social grouping the method enables us to discover any special tendencies for the people of certain divisions to intermarry, tendencies which may perhaps not have been noticed by the people themselves. The method renders possible the exact study of such forms of marriage as polygyny and polyandry, the levirate and cross-cousin marriage. These institutions have many variations which easily escape attention by the ordinary methods of inquiry but which become perfectly clear when their nature is worked out in detail from the pedigrees. Further, the method enables us to detect how far the marriage regulations of a people are being actually followed in practice, and a study of the marriages in successive generations may reveal a progressive change in the strictness with which any given regulation has been observed. It is indeed possible to work out the most complex problems concerned in the regulation of marriage without having ever asked a direct question on the matter, though it is not desirable to do this, for one of the most interesting features of the genealogical method is furnished by the comparison of the results gained by the genealogical method with those derived from direct inquiry. If there are discrepancies between the two the investigation of these may not only give the clue to new points of view but much light may be thrown on the linguistic or psychological peculiarities which have been the cause of the misunderstanding.

The sample pedigree from Guadalcanal is too small to furnish a good example of the application of the method, but it will be noticed that in no case have two people of the same clan married and that out of a total of eight marriages, four have taken place between members of the Kindapalei and Lakwili clans, a fact which is probably explained by the existence of the cross-cousin marriage in that island. It also furnishes one example of marriage with a member of another community, viz., with a native of the neighbouring island of Savo, the clans of which correspond closely to those of Guadalcanal.

The next line of application of the method is in the investigation of the laws regulating descent and the inheritance of property. Thus in the sample pedigree it will be seen that each person belongs to the clan of his mother, thus illustrating the matrilineal descent of this part of the Solomon Islands. The mode of succession of chiefs can be exactly studied in the same manner, while the method is especially important in the study of the inheritance of property. Thus it is possible to take a given piece of land and inquire into its history, perhaps from the time when it was first cultivated. The history of its divisions and sub-divisions on various occasions may be minutely followed, and a case of ownership which would seem hopelessly complicated becomes perfectly simple and intelligible in the light of its history, and an insight is given into the real working of the laws concerning property which could never be obtained by any less concrete method.

Another line of application which is occasionally of great value is in the study of migrations. Thus in many parts of Melanesia there has taken place during the last fifty years a change from life in the bush to life on the sea-coast, and the information given by the localities of successive generations may throw much light on the nature of such a migration.

The uses so far considered are concerned with the study of social organization, but the method is not without its uses in the study of magic and religion. In most of the people studied by myself it has been found that very definite functions in ceremonial are assigned to people who stand in certain relationships either to the performer of the ceremony or to the person on whose behalf it is being carried out. I believe that the exact inquiry rendered possible by the genealogical method would show that these functions connected with relationship are far more general than current anthropological literature would lead us to suppose, and further that the duties or privileges of kin discovered in this manner can be much more closely defined. The method enables one also to investigate ceremonial much more concretely than would otherwise be possible. When I am working at this subject I have my book of pedigrees by my side, and as I obtain the names of the various participants I look them out and see how they are related to the performer or subject of the ceremony, and at the same time there is the advantage that these become real personages to me although I may never have seen them, and the whole investigation proceeds in a manner which interests both me and my informants far more than if the personages in the account had been X, Y and Z.

Still another large group of uses to which the method can be put is in the study of many problems which, though they are primarily biological, are yet of great sociological importance. I refer to such matters as the proportion of the sexes, the size of the family, the sex of the first-born child, the proportion of children who grow up and marry to the total number born, and other similar subjects which can be studied statistically by the genealogical method. We have in the pedigrees a large mass of data of the utmost value for the exact study of various demographic problems, but in this connection it is necessary to utter a note of warning. In my experience the memories of the people are less trustworthy in regard to the children of past generations who have died young or before marriage than in the case of those who have married and had offspring. It is obvious that the latter will have gained social importance which has made the preservation of their names natural, while it is less to be expected that those who have died young or unmarried should be so perpetuated. It has often been surprising to me that the latter are remembered as well as they are, but there can be little doubt that some must be forgotten, and that statistics concerning these more biological matters are less complete than those dealing with the more strictly social problems.

Still another most important use of the method is as an aid to physical anthropology. As an example of this I cannot do better than give the instance of an island visited by Mr Hocart and myself last year where there are two constant sources of inter-mixture, in both cases with people whose physical characters are decidedly different from those of the general mass of the inhabitants. The measurement of the population of that island by the ordinary methods can hardly have had any definite result, but by means of the genealogical method we were able to discover the immediate ancestry of each person we measured. Further, the combination of physical measurement with the use of the genealogical method provides a mass of material for the study of problems in heredity. The method also makes it possible to work out very completely the mode of inheritance of such conditions as colour-blindness and albinism which are present in varying proportion in most parts of the world.

Some incidental advantages of the genealogical method may be briefly mentioned. Much information may be gained concerning transmission of names, and in the sample pedigree it will be noticed that a child has been given the name of his great-grand-father. Further, the name of some dead person, perhaps one who may have lived a century ago, will recall a story of the old life of the people which would possibly otherwise not have been obtained, and chance remarks thrown out in connection with the names of ancestors in this way often furnish most valuable suggestions for inquiry. Further, the mere collection of names provided in the pedigrees forms a storehouse of linguistic material which would be of great value if it were not for the fact that we have too little knowledge of the more living parts of the language to enable it to be utilized.

Having now considered the more detailed lines of inquiry in which the genealogical method is useful or essential, I proceed to sum up briefly some of its advantages in more general terms. In the first place I would mention its concreteness. Everyone who knows people of low culture must recognize the difficulty which besets the study of any abstract question, not so much because the savage does not possess abstract ideas as that he has no words of his own to express them, while he certainly cannot be expected to appreciate properly the abstract terms of the language of his visitor or of any other foreign language which serves as the means of communication. The genealogical method makes it possible to investigate abstract problems on a purely concrete basis. It is even possible by its means to formulate laws regulating the lives of people which they have probably never formulated themselves, certainly not with the clearness and definiteness which they have to the mind trained by a more complex civilization. Endless misunderstandings are avoided which are liable to arise between people from such different spheres, misunderstandings which have their source in differences of outlook and in the lack of appreciation on one side or other of the niceties of the language, whether European or native, which is serving as the means of communication. The method cannot do away with the difficulties which beset the interpretation of the social conditions of the savage by the visitor from another civilization, but it gives a mass of definite and indubitable facts to be interpreted.

From this point of view the method is more particularly useful to those who, like myself, are only able to visit savage or barbarous peoples for comparatively short times, times wholly insufficient to acquire that degree of mastery over the native language to enable it to be used as the instrument of intercourse. To such the method is essential if there is to be any hope of getting facts of real value about the more complex features of social organization. By means of the genealogical method it is possible, with no knowledge of the language and with very inferior interpreters, to work out with the utmost accuracy systems of kinship so complicated that Europeans who have spent their whole lives among the people have never been able to grasp them. It is not an exaggeration to say that in such a matter as this or in that of the regulation of marriage, it is possible by this method to obtain more definite and exact knowledge than is possible without it to a man who has lived for many years among the people and has obtained as full a knowledge as is ever acquired by a European of the language of a savage or barbarous people.

Another great general advantage of the method is that it gives one the means of testing the accuracy of one's witnesses. Among savages just as among ourselves there are the greatest differences between persons in the accuracy with which they can give an account of a ceremony or describe the history of a person or course of events. The genealogical method gives one a ready means of testing this accuracy. I do not mean merely that a person who

H

remembers pedigrees accurately will probably have an accurate memory on other subjects, but that the concrete method of inquiry which the genealogical method renders possible enables one to detect carelessness and inaccuracy so much more readily than is possible by the more ordinary methods of inquiry. It is not an unimportant point that the knowledge that the facts are accurate gives one a sense of comfort in one's work which is no small asset in the trying conditions, climatic and otherwise, in which most anthropological work has to be done. Further, the genealogical method not only gives one confidence in one's witnesses but it has an effect perhaps quite as important in giving the savage confidence in his questioner. Everyone knows the old statement that the chief characteristic of the savage is that he will tell you whatever you want to know. When he does this it is because it seems to him the easiest way of getting through a task in which he takes no interest, often because he does not understand the real nature of the questions, but I believe often because he recognizes that his questioner does not himself understand them. What seem to be the most simple questions to the uninstructed European may as a matter of fact be quite incapable of a straightforward answer, and it is not surprising that the puzzled child of nature should take the easiest way of ending the matter. I believe that the genealogical method puts the European inquirer on much the same footing as the native himself. It is quite certain that people of low culture would not preserve their pedigrees with the minuteness which is found to be the case if they were not of great practical importance in their lives, and the familiarity of his questioner with the instrument which he uses himself gives the savage confidence and interest in the inquiry which are of inestimable importance in getting information of real value. Further, the mutual confidence which is engendered by the use of the genealogical method in working out social organization extends to other departments of anthropology, and is not merely limited in its effects to the former.

Another very valuable feature of the genealogical method to which I have already referred is the help it gives in enabling us to understand those features of savage psychology which give anthropological work its difficulties. I am always in the habit of inquiring into matters both by the genealogical method and by the ordinary method of question and answer. There will often be discrepancies, and the investigation of these discrepancies often gives the most valuable insight into the mental peculiarities which have been the cause of the misunderstanding.

In conclusion there are two advantages of the method which are of so much importance that they would, to my mind, be sufficient to make its use essential even if there were no others.

It is almost impossible at the present time to find a people whose culture, beliefs and practices are not suffering from the effects of European influence, an influence which has been especially active during the last fifty years. To my mind the greatest merit of the genealogical method is that it often takes us back to a time before this influence had reached the people. It may give us records of marriage and descent and other features of social organization one hundred and fifty years ago, while events a century old may be obtained in abundance in all the communities with whom I have myself worked, and I believe that with proper care they could be obtained from nearly every people. Further, the course of the pedigrees is itself sometimes sufficient to demonstrate the gradual effect of the new influences which have affected the people.

The other pre-eminent merit of the method is that it gives us the means not merely of obtaining information but of demonstrating the truth of this information. Up till recently ethnology has been an amateur science. The facts on which the science has been based have been collected by people who have usually had no scientific training, and they have been imparted to the world with nothing to guarantee their accuracy or their completeness. It is a striking tribute to the essential veracity of the savage that these records are as good as they are, but anyone who has examined critically the records of any people must have found enormous diversities of evidence, and must have recognized that the records give in themselves no criteria which enable him to distinguish the false from the true. By means of the genealogical method it is possible to demonstrate the facts of social organization so that they carry conviction to the reader with as much definiteness as is possible in any biological science. The genealogical and other similar methods which render such demonstration possible will go far towards putting ethnology on a level with other sciences.

LIST OF WORKS CITED IN THE
INTRODUCTION AND COMMENTARIES

Abbreviations: *A.A.*   *American Anthropologist*
                 J.R.A.I. *Journal Royal Anthropological Institute*

BARNES, J. A., 1961. Physical and social kinship. *Philosophy of Science*, **28**, pp. 296–9.

BEATTIE, J. H. M., 1964. Kinship and Social Anthropology. *Man*, **64**, 130.

BOAS, F., 1911. *The Mind of Primitive Man*, New York.

CODRINGTON, R. H., 1891. *The Melanesians*, Oxford.

DURKHEIM, E., 1898. Zur Urgeschichte der Ehe, Prof. J. Kohler. *L'Année Sociologique*, **I**, pp. 306–19.

EGGAN, F. (Ed.), 1955. *Social Anthropology of North American Tribes*, Second Ed., Chicago.

EMMENEAU, M. B., 1941. Language and Social Forms, a Study of Toda Kinship Terms and Dual Descent. In *Language, Culture and Personality, essays in memory of Edward Sapir* (L. Spier, Ed.), Menasha, Wis.

FATHAUER, G. H., 1961. Trobriand. In *Matrilineal Kinship* (D. M. Schneider and K. Gough, Eds.), Berkeley and Los Angeles.

FIRTH, RAYMOND, 1936. *We, the Tikopia*, London.

—— 1958. *Social Anthropology as Science and as Art*, Dunedin.

FORTES, M., 1953. *Social Anthropology at Cambridge since 1900*, Cambridge.

—— 1957. Malinowski and the Study of Kinship. In *Man and Culture* (R. Firth, Ed.), London.

FORTUNE, R. F., 1932. *Sorcerers of Dobu*, London.

GELLNER, E., 1957. Ideal Language and Kinship Structure. *Philosophy of Science*, **24**, pp. 235–42.

—— 1960. The Concept of Kinship. *Philosophy of Science*, **27**, pp. 187–204.

—— 1963. Nature and Society in Social Anthropology. *Philosophy of Science*, **30**, pp. 236–51.

GIFFORD, E. W., 1922. *California Kinship Terminologies*. University of California Publications in American Archaeology and Ethnology, **18**.

GINSBERG, M., 1924. The Sociological Work of the late Dr W. H. R. Rivers. *Psyche*, **5**, pp. 33–52.

HERSKOVITS, M. J., 1948. *Man and His Works*, New York.

JOSSELIN DE JONG, J. P. B. DE, 1952. *Lévi-Strauss's Theory on Kinship and Marriage*, Leiden.

JULIUS, C. 1960. Malinowski's Trobriand Islands. *Journal of the Public Service, Territory of Papua and New Guinea,* **II**, Nos. 1 and 2.

KOHLER, J., 1897. Zur Urgeschichte der Ehe. *Zeitschrift für vergleichende Rechtswissenschaft*, **12**, pp. 187–353.

KROEBER, A. L., 1909. Classificatory Systems of Relationship. *J.R.A.I.*, **39**, pp. 77–84.

—— 1917. *California Kinship Systems*, University of California Publications in American Archaeology and Ethnology, **12**.

—— 1952. *The Nature of Culture*, Chicago.

LEACH, E. R., 1958. Concerning Trobriand Clans and the Kinship Category *Tabu*. In *The Developmental Cycle in Domestic Groups* (J. Goody, Ed.), Cambridge.

—— 1961. The Structural Implications of Matrilineal Cross-Cousin Marriage. In *Rethinking Anthropology*, London. (First published 1951, *J.R.A.I.*, **81**.)

LÉVI-STRAUSS, C., 1949. *Les Structures élémentaires de la parenté*, Paris.

LOUNSBURY, F. G., 1965. Another View of Trobriand Kinship Categories. *A.A.*, **67**, No. 5, Part 2, pp. 142–85.

LOWIE, R. H., 1920. *Primitive Society*, New York.

MALINOWSKI, B., 1913. *The Family among the Australian Aborigines*, London.

—— 1932. *The Sexual Life of Savages*. Third Ed., London.

MCLENNAN, J. F., 1876. *Studies in Ancient History*, London.

MORGAN, L. H., 1871. *Systems of Consanguinity and Affinity of the Human Family*. Smithsonian Contributions to Knowledge, **17**, Washington.

MURDOCK, G. P., 1949. *Social Structure*, New York.

NADEL, S. F., 1951. *The Foundations of Social Anthropology*, London.

NEEDHAM, R., 1962. *Structure and Sentiment*, Chicago.

POWELL, H. A., 1960. Competitive Leadership in Trobriand Political Organization. *J.R.A.I.*, **90**, pp. 118–45.

RADCLIFFE-BROWN, A. R., 1952. The Study of Kinship Systems. In *Structure and Function in Primitive Society*, London (First published 1941, *J.R.A.I.*, **71**.)

REAY, M., 1963. Review of Uberoi (1962). *Oceania*, **33**, pp. 296–8.

RIVERS, W. H. R., 1901–8. Vision; Genealogies; Kinship; etc. *Cambridge Anthropological Expedition to Torres Straits. Reports*, vols. II, V, VI. Cambridge.

—— 1906. *The Todas*, London.

—— 1907. On the Origin of the Classificatory System of Relationships. In *Anthropological Essays presented to Edward Burnett Tylor*, Oxford.

—— 1910a. The Genealogical Method of Anthropological Inquiry. *The Sociological Review*, **3**, pp. 1–12. (Reprinted here pp. 97–109.)

—— 1910b. The Father's Sister in Oceania. *Folklore*, **21**, pp. 42–59.

—— 1914a. *Kinship and Social Organisation*, London. (Reprinted here pp. 39–96.)

—— 1914b. *The History of Melanesian Society*, 2 vols., Cambridge.

—— 1914c. Kin, Kinship. *Encyclopaedia of Religion and Ethics* (James Hastings, Ed.), Edinburgh.

—— 1915. Marriage (Introductory and Primitive). *Encyclopaedia of Religion and Ethics* (James Hastings, Ed.), Edinburgh.

—— 1932. *Conflict and Dream*, Second Ed., London.

ROBINSON, M., 1962. Complementary Filiation and Marriage in the Trobriand Islands: a Re-examination of Malinowski's Material. In *Marriage in Tribal Societies* (M. Fortes, Ed.), Cambridge.

SCHNEIDER, D. M., 1964. The Nature of Kinship. *Man*, **64**, 217.

—— 1965. The Content of Kinship. Letter, *Man*, **65**, 108.

——1965b. American Kin Terms and Terms for Kinsmen: A Critique of Yankee Kinship Terminology. *A.A.* **67**, No. 5, Part 2, pp. 288-308.

——(in press) *American Kinship: A Cultural Account.* Chigago.

SIDER, K.B. 1967. Kinship and Culture: Affinity and the Role of a Father in the Trobriands. *Southwestern Journal of Anthropology,* **23**, pp. 90-109.

STARCKE, C. N., 1889. *The Primitive Family: Its Origin and Development,* London.

TAX, S., 1955. From 'Lafitau to Radcliffe-Brown: A Short History of the Study of Social Organizations'. In F. Eggan (Ed.), 1955, pp. 445-84.

THOMAS, N. W., 1906. *Kinship Organisations and Group Marriage in Australia,* Cambridge.

TYLOR, E. B., 1889. On a Method of Investigating the Development of Institutions; applied to Laws of Marriage and Descent. *J.R.A.I.,* **18**, pp. 245-72.

UBEROI, J. P. SINGH, 1962. *Politics of the Kula Ring,* Manchester.

INDEX

LONDON SCHOOL OF ECONOMICS
MONOGRAPHS ON SOCIAL ANTHROPOLOGY

Titles marked with an asterisk are now out of print. Those marked with a dagger have been reprinted in paperback editions and are only available in this form.